WALKING IN DERBYSHIRE

A detailed route guide
for rambling in the Peak
District National Park
and adjacent countryside

Contributors:

J. W. ALLEN   CLARENCE DANIEL
JAMES DOBBY
KEITH MANTELL   FRANK RODGERS

Maps by CHARLES H. BROWN

Completely revised by H. MARTIN

Seventh revised edition

DERBYSHIRE COUNTRYSIDE LTD

Lodge Lane, Derby

ISBN 0 85100 069 X

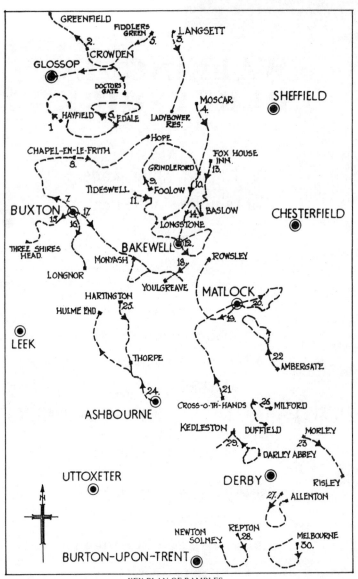

KEY PLAN OF RAMBLES

2

ROUTES

3

THE CONTRIBUTORS

J. W. ALLEN, F.G.S.—Historian and writer on wayside topics.

CLARENCE DANIEL—Writer on the folklore and historical associations of Eyam and district.

JAMES DOBBY—Journalist and mountaineer. Keenly interested in the open moorlands of the High Peak.

KEITH MANTELL—Librarian. Author of *Dovedale Guide* and *Melbourne Story,* and a former Editor of *Derbyshire Life and Countryside*—the county magazine.

FRANK RODGERS—Writer and photographer with extensive portfolio of Derbyshire scenes.

FOREWORD

SINCE the death of Mr. James Haworth, who was General Editor and did so much for previous editions of this booklet, all the walks have been personally checked by Mr. Herbert Martin for this new edition. There have been quite a few changes even in three years. This is because of the rapid development of new farming techniques, the loss of hedgerows and extensive prairie ploughing.

Because of the increase in carelessness amongst the public and the incidence of vandalism, farmers are becoming more wary of people crossing their land, and if they sometimes get upset one should feel sympathetic towards them.

As in previous editions, the route guides are so arranged in *Walking in Derbyshire* that they commence at a point beyond the northern boundaries of the county and follow a loosely-drawn pattern through the High Peak and Mid-Derbyshire to the plains of the Trent Valley in the south. The arrangement is not intended to convey some personal preference for one particular area over another, but merely to offer a convenient and orderly presentation to those who will find the booklet a useful and helpful guide to their rambling excursions in the county. Each walk described is independent of its neighbour in the preceding or following pages, whether they are complementary to a particular area or not.

Every care has been exercised in compiling the walks, but adjustments do occasionally occur within months of a survey being undertaken. The Editor would, therefore be grateful for any information from ramblers who may discover alterations which have occurred in the meantime and which are not in keeping with the text or drawn maps.

It should be clearly understood that the representation in the text of the route directions—or in any of the maps—of the existence of a road, track or footpath does not necessarily indicate that a right-of-way exists with free passage to everyone. Where, however, good manners and commonsense prevail, there is usually no objection to passing over land where there are indications of a footpath being available.

A COUNTY OF DIVERSE SCENERY

THERE is something altogether irresistible about Derbyshire, for once the charm of its renowned scenic beauty has been experienced a feeling of uninhibited pleasure is retained throughout one's lifetime.

Indeed, it is the diversity of scenic change which lends enchantment to all that is best in Derbyshire. Differences in the earth's crust—and flora—are nowhere more noticeable than when observed between areas of millstone grit and the lighter shades of mountain limestone.

On the one hand there are the forbidding shale and sandstone outcrops to be found around Froggatt, Stanage and Rushup Edges, while on the other there is the magic land of caverns, disappearing rivers and enchanting wooded valleys which are riddled with lead and other minerals. The coal measures, too, along the eastern boundary and in the south of the county have their pleasant surprises as well as their eyesores.

Daniel Defoe, who wrote scathingly of the Peak district in his eighteenth-century *Tour of England and Wales*—he called it "a houling wilderness"—would be astonished at the assumption that people, seeking escape from urbanised surroundings, are attracted in ever-increasing numbers to this "houling wilderness"—just for the sake of feeling the wind on their cheeks when enjoying the thrill of "going over the tops".

It is not always recognised that eighteenth-century landowners made worthwhile contributions to the preservation of the English countryside. It was their influence, in addition to their wealth, which saved the Derbyshire landscape from industrial spoliation, even if their motives were not always directed from the standpoint of public well-being.

During the twentieth century, however, there has been a remarkable change in outlook, for many far-sighted individuals have made outstanding benefactions towards preserving the amenities of the countryside.

Sir Robert McDougall and Mr. F. A. Holmes were two distinguished men among others who presented large tracts of land in Dovedale and the Manifold Valley to the National Trust—so that many hundreds of acres of this lovely area could be made safe for all time for the enjoyment of the public.

The National Trust, too, has made its own outstanding contributions to preserving vast stretches of these remarkable limestone dales, for it is the owner of hundreds of acres of woodland in Dovedale and the immediate neighbourhood as well as in other parts of Derbyshire.

All these efforts—complementary to each other in an overall endeavour to preserve the countryside—helped to lay the foundations for the Peak District National Park, which is not merely a defined area on a map but a real park where people can enjoy themselves.

Admittedly, there are rules to be observed, for in a tight little island such as the United Kingdom — where good agricultural land is at a premium—there are no heaven-sent opportunities for unrestricted camping as and when one may feel inclined. A landowner's fences and growing crops are still respected. There are, however, ample alternative means for enjoying the great outdoors by way of Youth Hostels and wayside inns. Camping sites are available, of course, if only in a restricted form.

The landscape alone is not the full extent of Derbyshire's bounty by any means, for in some of the smaller towns, such as Ashbourne, Buxton, Bakewell or Matlock, there are pleasant diversions at hand. Many of the villages, too, are endowed with churches and manor houses of outstanding architectural interest and possess historic monuments which arouse the keen investigations of many visitors.

There are no old cathedrals in the county, but there are six great country houses which attract thousands of visitors every spring and summer. They are:

CHATSWORTH HOUSE, near Bakewell; HADDON HALL, near Bakewell; HARDWICK HALL, eight miles south-east of Chesterfield; MELBOURNE HALL, eight miles south of Derby; KEDLESTON HALL, four miles north-west of Derby; and SUDBURY HALL, six miles east of Uttoxeter on the A50.

These showplaces of the county are well worth a visit but check for dates and times of opening.

Derbyshire has much to offer those who would seek out its bounteous offerings. The pleasures to be derived from exploring the countryside will not only stimulate the body by health-giving exercise, but will readily afford an opportunity for refreshing the mind when seeking peace and contentment among the hills and dales.

Hayfield, Lantern Pike, Mount Famine, Edale

L EAVE Hayfield passing the church on your left, turning left into Bank Street, then sharp left past the Post Office to river-side path passing under new by-pass bridge. Follow the embankment to road. Turn left passing school and keeping left up to a row of houses. Turn sharp right along frontage and bear left through stile, following the path always up and left through a gulley which emerges on the ridge of Lantern Pike. Continue forward and, bearing right again, a six-armed signpost is soon reached. A steep descent to the right leads directly to the main Glossop road again, completing a horseshoe.

Half a mile to the north up the Glossop road, a bridle road to Edale is reached on the right and the path over the bridge leads out over the moor to descend to Hayfield reservoir, a good point for "halving" the walk if you so desire.

Otherwise, follow the track on the left bank of the river towards Hayfield and then take the left path upwards from the fork and ascend Mount Famine.

Keep the twin peaks of South Head on the right until you join the little road leading down into Roych Clough. Here, a steep climb near the western entrance of the Cowburn Tunnel on the Dore and Chinley railway line takes one along a footpath leading to the main Chapel-Castleton road.

A short distance towards Castleton we find a signposted footpath running inside the wall on our left and follow this for 300 yards. We then turn left across Peatlands and, taking the right fork a little farther on, swing steeply down the ancient Chapel Gate to Barber Booth.

Our path emerges at a point where there is refreshment before the last mile to Edale station, where we can join trains for either Chinley or Sheffield.

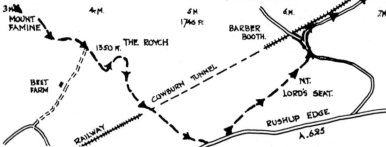

8

Crowden, Chew Reservoir, Greenfield

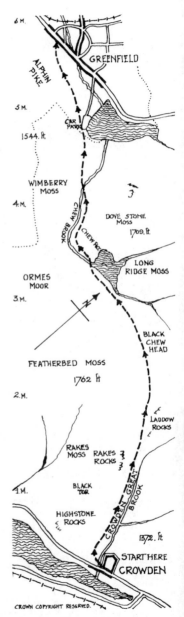

MANY valleys in the Peak District National Park have been inundated to provide water for nearby cities, but to traverse a footpath linking three of the more northern reservoirs provides one of the best excursions in the north-western area of the park. The valleys of Longdendale, Chew and Greenfield are best approached by bus from Barnsley, Manchester or Sheffield, alighting at Crowden. Here, is the Pennine Way Hostel, built by the Peak Park Planning Board, providing overnight accommodation for the week-ender and refreshment for the day walker.

Our route is the footpath avoiding the Crowden rifle range, following along the left (west) side of the iron fence until the rough path strikes higher ground, passing on its way the dripping face of Rake's Rocks. In the distance, the profile of Laddow Rocks comes into view, often with the interlaced ropes of rock climbers spread across the craggy wall of the rock face. The walker's way, however, is not to the foot of the rocks, but to follow the steep path up the brook to the top of the outcrop and then swing away westwards. Ahead, the skyline is dominated by Black Hill over which the Pennine Way winds on its way to Scotland.

The ancient trackway we are following is well marked by massive cairns. The deepest peat troughs in Peakland lie to our right.

By the Chew reservoir, Chew House and Chew Brook we must walk for two miles or so over extremely rough ground before reaching, with some sense of relief, the waterworks house and steep incline which is the beginning of our descent into the valley.

Here, yet another reservoir confronts us and care has to be taken in traversing around the embankment to reach, finally, the little road which leads us out on to the main Holmfirth-Greenfield (Isle of Skye) road to Greenfield itself and the bus for our return journey.

For those requiring overnight accommodation near the commencement of the walk there is the Peak National Park Hostel. It is also suitable for a weekend, or longer, stay as a centre for exploring the nearby moorlands. The Hostel address is: The Warden, Peak National Park Hostel, Crowden, Hadfield, Hyde, Cheshire. Tel. Glossop 2135.

9

Flouch Inn (or Langsett), Cut Gate, Back Tor, Ladybower

WHERE the counties of Yorkshire and Derbyshire meet in the north-west corner of the Peak District National Park, lies perhaps the more renowned of our northern dales and one of the best of all millstone edges—that of Derwent.

The Flouch Inn, or Langsett, the choice of starting points, are best reached by bus from Barnsley, Sheffield or Manchester. The bus stop in the case of the former, is the Flouch cross-roads, from where we retrace our way up the main road for 50 yards towards Manchester. By a small cottage on our left, a footpath sign points the way through a small plantation to the Porter (or Little) Don River.

At the bridge over the river, we are joined by the path from the inn at Langsett which has wound through the plantation at the side of the reservoir to join up at the bridge. Crossing the bridge, we are faced immediately with a short, but tremendously steep climb.

This first real call on wind and muscle brings us to the eastern side of Hingcliff Hill and, rounding this, we drop down to the foot of Mickledean Edge. Here begins the long, steady climb by the side of Bull Clough, the main stream. At the point where the Clough joins parallel with our track, we walk to the left of its mouth then swing right and again left along the peaty Black Dike which forms the ancient Cut Gate bridleway, used within living memory by farmers from Derwent Woodlands on their journeys to and from Penistone market. Continuing to the summit at 1,724 feet, we strike left for about a third of a mile to the stake at the top of Margery Hill (1,793 feet).

Proceeding along the ridge and the border of National Trust property, we keep clear of the groughs on our left, which would take us down to the Ewden Valley and, later, avoid the deep cut of Abbey Brook on the right, which would mean a descent into the Derwent Valley.

By Howshaw Tor, Back Tor and Derwent Edge's long line, with its outcrop of fascinating names like Cakes of Bread and the Salt Cellar, we also pass the Wheel Stones—another outcrop half a mile to the south-east and known locally as the Coach and Horses. For the rock

10

climber, these provide ideal "boulder problems", but for the winter walker they are invaluable shelters from cutting winds while a midday meal is consumed.

Near the Wheel Stones, we leave the Edge to find the footpath which drops easily at first, and then more steeply, into the valley and the road (A57) by the Ladybower Inn, with its bus stop for Sheffield. Another two miles away is Bamford and railway links with Sheffield or Manchester.

ALTERNATIVE—By starting at Strines Bottom, a distance less than the eleven miles is involved and this setting-off point on the A57 is reached by alighting from the bus from Sheffield at the junction with the Moscar and Strines road and walking down past the inn to the start of the footpath in the middle bend of the reservoir.

All these are ancient ways—perhaps the oldest of all in Peakland. Access is still disputed in places and public ways, marked by signposts, should be followed.

A recommendation for this walk—one that hardly needs stressing—is that, under ideal weather conditions, the views obtainable on the Cut Gate route are truly rewarding. The inexperienced, however, should not venture out unaccompanied, for the weather can change abruptly in these parts.

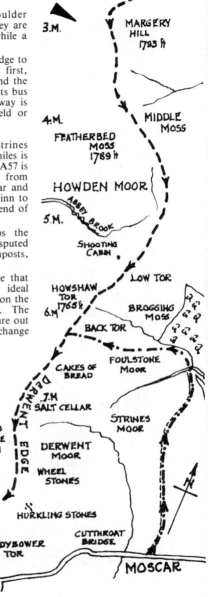

MARGERY HILL 1793 ft

3.M.

MIDDLE MOSS

4.M.

FEATHERBED MOSS 1789 ft

HOWDEN MOOR

ABBEY BROOK

5.M.

SHOOTING CABIN

LOW TOR

HOWSHAW TOR 1765 ft

6.M.

BROGGING MOSS

BACK TOR

FOULSTONE MOOR

CAKES OF BREAD

DERWENT EDGE

SALT CELLAR

STRINES MOOR

HIGH HO GRINDLE BARN

DERWENT MOOR

WHEEL STONES

8.M.

CROOK HILL

HURKLING STONES

CUTTHROAT BRIDGE

LADYBOWER TOR

LADYBOWER RES.

MOSCAR

N

9.M.

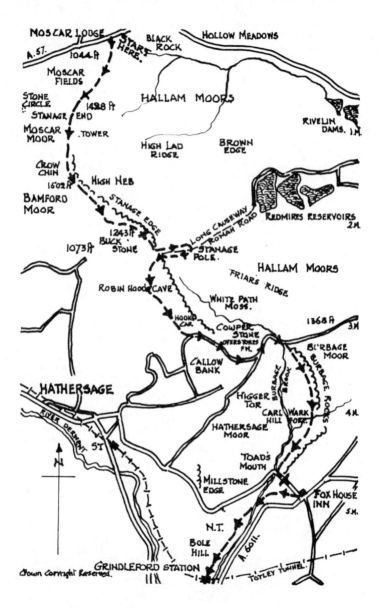

MOSCAR LODGE BLACK ROCK HOLLOW MEADOWS
A.57 1044 ft START HERE.
MOSCAR FIELDS
STONE CIRCLE 1428 ft
STANAGE END HALLAM MOORS
MOSCAR MOOR .TOWER RIVELIN DAMS. 1 M.
HIGH LAD RIDGE BROWN EDGE
CROW CHIN HIGH NEB
1502 ft
BAMFORD MOOR STANAGE EDGE LONG CAUSEWAY
REDMIRES RESERVOIRS
ROMAN ROAD 2 M.
1073 ft 1243 ft STANAGE POLE
BUCK STONE HALLAM MOORS
FRIAR'S RIDGE
ROBIN HOOD CAVE WHITE PATH MOSS.
HOOK'S CAR 1368 ft 3 M.
COWPER STONE
OVERSTONES FM.
CALLOW BANK BURBAGE MOOR
BURBAGE BROOK BURBAGE ROCKS
HATHERSAGE HIGGER TOR 4 M.
RIVER DERWENT CARL WARK FORT
CARL HILL
ST HATHERSAGE MOOR
TOAD'S MOUTH
MILLSTONE EDGE FOX HOUSE INN
N 5 M.
N.T. A.6011
BOLE HILL
GRINDLEFORD STATION TOTLEY TUNNEL
Crown Copyright Reserved.

12

Moscar, Stanage Edge, Fox House, Grindleford Station

STAND on Kinder Scout and look east, or stand on Derwent Edge and look south. Stand anywhere on the higher contours of the Peak District and always you will see a long grey line beckoning you: STANAGE. Stanage is renowned for its rock climbs, for its cave, and for the views it affords of the valleys that fall away below.

We approach Stanage from the main Sheffield-Manchester (A57) road, via Moscar. Bus services from Sheffield and, also, at less frequent intervals from Bakewell, are our best means of getting to the start of our track, which is almost on the Derbyshire-Yorkshire boundary. Here, we leave the road at the public footpath sign to trek upwards and across the higher wastes of Hallam Moors to Stanage itself.

An ancient bridle road takes us beneath the rocks and would lead us down to Hathersage if we wished, or we could join the path dropping down to Bamford. For our walk, however, we pass just below the rocks to join the Roman Causeway taking us to the top of the outcrop at Stanage Pole.

To the north-east of this point, the 1,457 feet mark, is a stone-paved road believed by some to have been the connecting link between the major Roman camp at Brough, near Hope, and the lesser camps at Temple-borough, near Rotherham, and Wincobank Hill, Sheffield. Others claim the pavement is merely an 18th century road used to convey millstones from the Stanage quarries to Sheffield.

From the Pole, which serves as a boundary mark between the two counties, we can enjoy, on a clear day, some of the finest views obtainable in the Peak District. These range from Bleaklow Head in the west, down Derwent Vale to the dams, with Ladybower tucked away beneath us.

Returning from our lookout at the Pole to the main route once again, we pass beneath the edge on our left as we face outward from the rocks, slightly retracing our steps until we weave our way leftwards round under the rocks again, noticing on our right the new car park and picnic area of Hollin Bank. Then on to the lane past Overstones Farm.

For those whose way home lies through Sheffield, it is easy from here to reach transport. But for us the way is by the green pathway beneath Burbage Rocks, which we find on our right as we branch off down the road to Ringinglow. From this pathway, we see majestic Higger Tor on the right and the path by Burbage Brook is comforting to the feet after the boulder-strewn slopes beneath Stanage.

The way is clear — a satisfying, end-of-the-day wander down to the Hathersage road. If we turn left up the road for 400 yards or so we come to Fox House Inn and transport to Sheffield, Bakewell and Buxton. Alternatively we can cross the road and cross and recross the murmuring Burbage Brook as, in company with it, we thread our way through the beautiful greenery of Padley Woods to Grindleford Station.

The woods, especially in springtime, abound in rewarding pursuits for the nature lover and birdwatcher, for there is some new revelation to be experienced with every other twist in the track as one leisurely descends on Grindleford railway station.

Fiddlers Green, Bleaklow, Snake Pass

THE northern boundaries of the Peak District National Park are marked by great areas of heath and moorland bog of no particular use for agricultural purposes other than sheep grazing.

The topography of the area may easily be envisaged from the very name of the place: BLEAKLOW. Bordered in the east by the Sheffield-Manchester road and in the west by the town of Glossop and the "new" road to Crowden, Bleaklow is a formidable plateau containing probably the second largest area of trackless moorland country in the British Isles. The Barnsley-Manchester road contains the area in the north while the Snake Pass in the south divides Bleaklow from its neighbour, Kinder Scout.

As with Kinder Scout, game rights are strictly preserved and during the shooting season the moors are closed to walkers on certain days of the week.

The less experienced fell walker would do well to think twice before venturing on the Bleaklow moors alone, for this is country where experience, first-rate equipment, and an ability to read maps and use a compass are essential.

Leaving the bus at the highest point of the Barnsley-Manchester road at Fiddlers Green, our route takes us up the old road to Lady Cross (look for the ancient cross in the small square of railings).

On a compass bearing south, we head for the 1,627 feet point and find before us Shepherds' Meeting Stones, unmarked even on the 1 in. Ordnance Survey map, but the scene of former gatherings when, once a year, Peakland shepherds met to sort out their flocks. A short descent into the upper

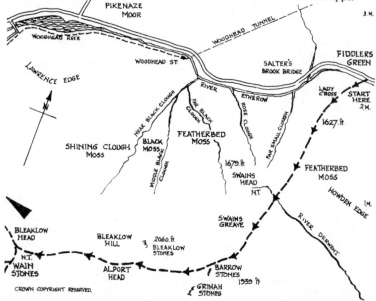

CROWN COPYRIGHT RESERVED.

14

reaches of the River Derwent and we are soon climbing up to Barrow Stones after crossing the stream. In fine weather, the westward trek across the plateau to Bleaklow Stones is easy, when the deepest peat groughs are avoided, but in bad weather constant reference to a compass is essential. Traversing Bleaklow Hill from the 2,060 feet point at Bleaklow Stones to the same height at Wain Stones, brings us on to the Pennine Way track, where a course along the Devil's Dike takes us down to the Snake road.

Those concerned with making use of public transport at the end of their walk may find alternative descents from Wain Stones to their advantage. So follow the Pennine Way track north-westward down the side of Torside Clough into Crowden, or west down Yellowslack Brook to join the Doctor's Gate Roman road track into Glossop.

Bleaklow is tough, demanding moorland country which calls for physical effort and skill when traversing these wild uplands. Care is necessary and one should not venture out alone—in case of accidents.

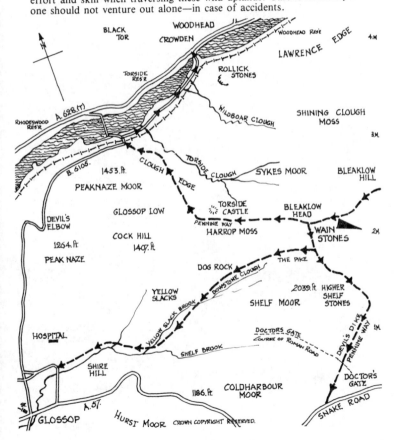

Edale, Kinder Scout, Crookstone Knoll, Edale

ON a first visit to the Peak District National Park many people look for a spot they have heard referred to as The Peak. What they eventually find is a high plateau—that of Kinder Scout itself, once forbidden territory.

Kinder is best approached by train to Edale where, on leaving the station, we turn left up the road. On our right is the new National Park Information Centre where advice, maps and guide books are always available. Our route starts from the timber bridge over Grindsbrook, reached by continuing beyond the Old Nag's Head Hotel to the point where a path drops steeply to the river and the bridge itself.

This, according to which way they are travelling, is either the start or the finish of the 250 mile-long Pennine Way route from Edale to the Scottish Border. A well-worn footpath across the meadows takes us over a stile, through a copse, over another stile and out on to the hillside, where we follow, at varying heights, along the side of the brook until, in a mile or so, we reach a fork in the stream. Proceeding up one or other stream takes one up to the edge of the plateau. Turning left (west) the Edge track is followed over Grindlow Knoll and on to Crowden Tower. Here, we have extensive views across the Valley of Edale, with the Lose Hill—Rushup Edge ridge in the foreground on our left.

Continuing by Edale Head and Noe Stool, we follow the plateau's edge track round to Swinesback (from afar it looks like one!) to Kinder Low. Half a mile to the north-east is the highest point in the whole of Peakland, "The Peak" on the old maps, at 2,088 feet.

With the west wind beating on our left cheek and panoramic views of Hayfield (a good starting place, too) below us, we are now heading for

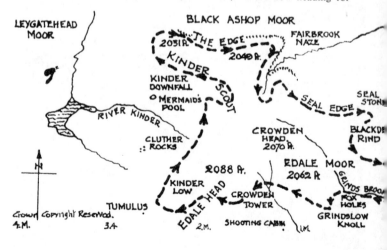

Kinder Downfall—a mere trickle of water over smooth rocks in summer, but a glorious cascade with rainbow sprays or a frozen mass of gleaming icicles in winter.

Resisting being tempted into bogs by inviting sheeptracks, we follow the track round the Edge to Fairbrook Naze, the steep escarpment overlooking both Ashop Clough and the Snake Pass, keeping the latter in view all the time now as we swing along by Seal Edge, Blackden Edge and Crookstone Knoll—the plateau's eastern limits. The plateau is almost a ridge in itself hereabouts and if the day is clear there are some notable landmarks to be seen: Bleaklow plateau unfolds across the Snake Road. To the right is Derwent Edge, with Ladybower Reservoir nestling in the valley. South-eastwards lie Win Hill and Bamford Edge.

It is time we were heading homewards and our path lies on the southern edge of the plateau—above the head of Lady Booth and Oller Brook—to where Golden Clough drops steeply away from Ringing Roger's shapely outcrop into a gliding descent back to Grindsbrook. We then rejoin our original path at the stile into the woods and back to Edale.

For those who traverse the whole round of this plateau, no less than 15 hard miles will lie behind them at the finish. The less ambitious need not be overawed by distances, however, for this circular walk can start and end at many of the points indicated. In addition to the Edale starting point, for instance, Hayfield and the Snake Road form equally good starting and finishing points, though it must be remembered that public transport on the latter road is almost non-existent.

Access points to the Kinder plateau are now numerous and are indicated by signs on the moorlands as well as on National Park maps to be found in many places in the district. During the shooting season, many of the upland moors are closed to walkers for one day a week—often a Monday—and the voluntary wardens who patrol the area will give advice as to alternative routes.

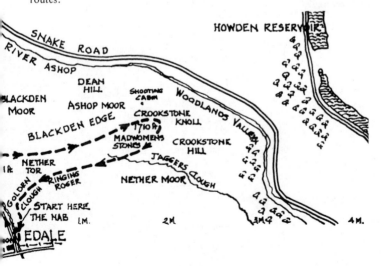

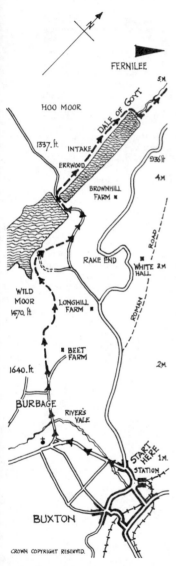

FERNILEE

HOO MOOR

DALE OF GOYT

5ᴍ

1337 ft. INTAKE

ERRWOOD

936 ft

4ᴍ

BROWNHILL
FARM ■

RAKE END

ROAD

WHITE 3ᴍ
HALL

WILD
MOOR
1470 ft.

LONGHILL
FARM ■

ROMAN

■ BEET
FARM

1640 ft.

2ᴍ

BURBAGE

RIVER'S
VALE

START
HERE 1ᴍ

STATION

BUXTON

CROWN COPYRIGHT RESERVED.

Buxton, Wild Moor, Fernilee, Taxal, Eccles Pike, Chapel

THIS walk commands views of areas which remain immune from industrialisation. From Buxton's sheltering hills, the way lies over Wild Moor to the milder scenery of the Goyt Valley.

We start from the Opera House in St. John's Road, Buxton, which we follow for a mile to Burbage. Instead of entering Burbage branch right into Bishop's Lane and into an unswerving stretch of road for a little more than half-a-mile, ignoring a first turning on the left. Continue forward for another 150 yards and then bear right up a rough lane and cross over a stile into a spinney about 75 yards above a cottage on the left, sign-posted 'Goyt Valley'.

Climb diagonally uphill but bear right as soon as you are through the wood. Make for the top right-hand corner of the field and negotiate the ladder stile over a stone wall. Turn right once over the wall and continue parallel with the wall until it is joined by a track climbing up from farm buildings down the hillside on the right. At this point turn sharp left across rough land to a solitary stoop marking a gateway near a broken-down sheepfold. Continue forward to the now abandoned High Peak Railway track, which can be seen curving round the hillside on the right.

Cross over the track (the rails have long since disappeared) and bear slight leftwards down the hillside and then bear right and follow the infant stream down into the clough. Move across the stream before the junction with one coming down from the left hand and mount the hillside and use the sheepwalks to proceed again downstream. Eventually we reach a newly-cut cart track, but continue downstream and breast the hillside by way of the new track to old Goyt Lane, which now disappears into the depths of Errwood Reservoir. Cross over the lane and move forward across a couple of fields and between fences, then take a right-hand incline up to the motor road, which dips left round Bunsal Cob to the reservoir embankment.

18

Having crossed over the embankment and enjoyed views both north and south, turn right downhill to the foot road leading along the left-hand shore of Fernilee Reservoir. At the northern end of Fernilee, cross the embankment to the opposite side of the reservoir and turn left downhill by the spillway to the waterworks buildings, where the path is resumed at the foot of steps passing the filter beds.

Ignoring the bridge over the river in the third field, continue along the path clinging to the riverside until a wood is entered by a stile. The way leads between the trees, but still keeps in close proximity with the river. Taxal Church (where the custom of rush-bearing was formerly observed) is seen across the river, at which point the path enters a narrow lane.

Here, turn right and climb steeply to cross the busy Buxton-Whaley road and up the lane on the opposite side. This lane turns left and straightens out to pass Shallcross Hall Farm. From this point, looking across the valley, we see the Roosdyche cleaving the opposite hill for three-quarters of a mile. This enigmatic valley was once thought to be a Roman chariot-way; later authorities thought it might be a worked out seam of coal; others that it is just a natural phenomenon. Continuing along the lane we reach a housing estate, and turn left down Elnor Lane to reach the Whaley-Chapel main road.

Cross the road and follow the Eccles Road over the railway bridge, turning right to continue up the lane for a mile or more and passing Ollerenshaw Hall and the hamlet of Hilltop.

Still climbing the lane up to Eccles Pike, we reach twin footpath signs on our right. Follow the top path, cutting across the field and keeping left across the next to a stile, and then proceed along the bottom of the next two fields. Ignoring a packhorse track cutting down to Bradshaw Hall on the right, the path continues some distance by a wall to reach a small copse through which we descend on our right to join the road, crossing the Chinley-Buxton road, to reach Chapel-en-le-Frith, the "Capital of the Peak".

Buxton is served by bus and limited rail services. There are frequent services for the return by bus from Chapel-en-le-Frith.

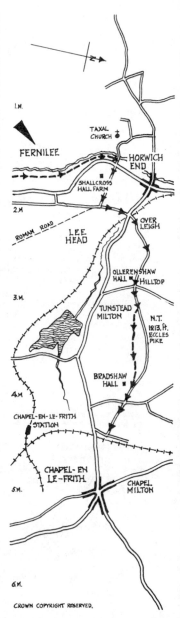

19

Chapel-en-le-Frith, Sparrowpit, Peak Forest, Cave Dale, Castleton, Brough, Hope

FROM Chapel-en-le-Frith, the capital of the Peak, we travel to the castle of Sir Walter Scott's "Peveril of the Peak" by way of a one-time Gretna Green where runaway marriages were solemnised. At Peak Forest is a church dedicated to Charles the Martyr and it was here, in the original chapel, that runaway couples were married. The initial stages of the walk, from Chapel to Peak Forest, can be dispensed with altogether if one is more favourably placed for a start at the halfway mark at Peak Forest.

Leaving Chapel-en-le-Frith market place, with its restored stocks, proceed downhill along the Buxton road (A624T), ignoring the twin turnings for Glossop and Castleton branching off left. Continue forward to the next left-hand turn and proceed into Blackbrook Lane and keep left at the next junction for the long climb uphill to Peaslows.

Once over the brow of the hill we drop down to Sparrowpit and its peculiarly named Wanted Inn, a wayside halt with a grill room view down to Barmoor Clough.

We proceed across the front of the inn along the A623 to Peak Forest, a couple of miles away. Almost opposite Peak Forest Church we turn left and continue past the Methodist Church, on the left, and go forward along a rutted lane when confronted with alternatives of turning left or right.

The lane peters out at a farm, but a short grass-covered track leads to a stile into a field, which we cross to a gap in the opposite wall. Straight across the next field there is a stile at the junction of three walls. Proceed up two fields by the wall on the left and up the next to a gap at the top, where we join a well-defined track near a pond.

The path bears right up the hillside, across a leadmine rake and then proceeds diagonally across a large field to the top end of the wall on the right. On the right of a gate in the far corner, a removable post gives access to a stile on your right. Now proceed along a grass track ahead with wall on your right. Rowter Farm, with Mam Tor as a backcloth, is seen away on the left, but proceed forward along the path, which is enclosed on either side as we approach a gate. A signpost here indicates a turn left to Castleton. The track crosses a field diagonally on a right incline

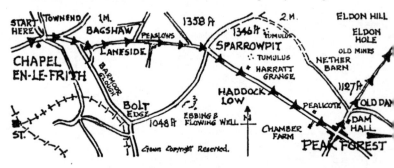

20

and then plunges into a dip, where we take a right fork to a stile leading down into Cave Dale.

We soon see the remains of the Norman keep of Peveril Castle on the heights above the dale. Ruined and incomplete though it is, there is sufficient structure remaining to make the steep walk up to the Castle Keep well worthwhile. In addition to the Keep much of the curtain wall survives, and within it the foundations of other buildings can be traced.

Another diversion before continuing the walk could be a visit to one of the more renowned caverns in the neighbourhood. There are five open to the public: Treak Cliff, Speedwell, Blue John, Treak Cliff Hill and Peak Cavern. The latter is quite close to the village and runs under the ruins of Peveril Castle.

In Castleton we turn down the road to Hope for about ¼ mile, turning right at a signpost just past the Police Station. A well-used path is plainly visible across Peakshole Water meadows before we cross a single-track railway line. We then traverse another four fields by the water's edge before entering Pindale Lane.

We can either terminate the walk here at Hope, or turn left for a few paces before turning right at the road junction for a short climb up to a stile (signposted) on our left for a visit to the Roman military station at Brough. We now proceed along a section of the grass-covered Roman road (Doctor's Gate) to a stile and turn left down the side of three fields and across to a step-stile. This takes us through the middle of a large field to cross a footbridge into the field containing the site of "Navio". The path cuts through the area occupied by the fort, with a few dressed stones marking the site of the Praetorium on our right. Proceed through two pillars identifying the original entrance, to a stile in the bottom right-hand corner. Turn left through Brough to the Traveller's Rest, where we may catch a bus, or turn left up to Hope Station.

Chapel has direct bus services from Buxton, Manchester and intermediate places with good connections. At Hope the Manchester-Castleton-Sheffield buses pass through the village and there is also a station on the Chinley-Sheffield (L.M.R.) line.

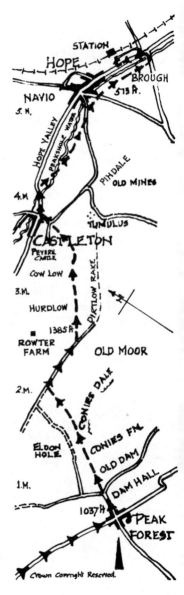

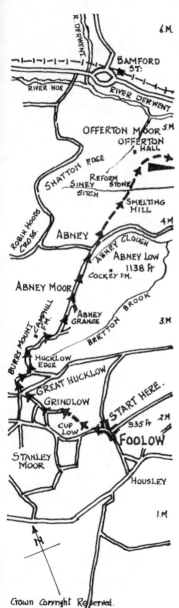

Foolow, Grindlow, Gt. Hucklow Abney, Hathersage, Grindleford

THE starting point is Foolow, a typical up-land village with church, chapel, inn, hall, and manor house encircling a green. We pass the playhouse of a one-time experiment in rural repertory, a gliding club, the halls of Offerton (with its cruck-built barn) and High-low, and Robin Hood's Stoop.

From Foolow we walk a short distance up the Tideswell road to enter a stile on the right, crossing three fields into a grass-covered lane which takes us into Grindlow. Continue forward along the road into Great Hucklow. Turn right opposite the Methodist Church. We pass the village school on our right before turning right up a sunken lane. Turning left at a stone pillar, we reach the road and continue left to the headquarters of the Derbyshire and Lancashire Gliding Club, at a spot where the road bends right.

Following the road, pass the cluster of Abney Grange farm on the right and descend into a glen which the road crosses into Abney. Over to the right we see Cockey Farm, birthplace of William Newton, the "Peak Minstrel". Proceeding through the hamlet, we climb a stile on our left (signposted: Public footpath to Offerton), bear left for 25 yards to another stile and continue uphill alongside the stone wall (on the right) for 100 yards. Here turn right and continue forward for another 75 yards to a step-ladder stile over another wall to the moor beyond.

Still ascending, the path weaves through bracken and heather, crossing a wall and fording a stream. We pass a cairn on our left and the path soon cuts through another. after which it begins to drop away, revealing a lovely view of the Derwent Valley.

Quickly descending, the pathway slants right along the hillside, and then splinters into innumerable outlets. Our goal is the gate at a point where the metalled road, approaching from the opposite direction, describes a sharp bend to reach Offerton Hall among the trees on the lower side.

Turning right along the road, a stone pillar on the right. This landmark is called

22

Robin Hood's Stoop and is probably an old boundary stone. Here there are alternative routes down to Hathersage. If you wish to see Highlow Hall, headquarters of the Eyre family, continue along the road which soon sweeps in a curve to join the Abney-Leadmill road, and turning right a short distance to the Hall. Returning down the road continue to the Plough Inn at Leadmill and turn left along the main road into Hathersage.

The alternative route turns left past the Stoop at a notice indicating Callow Farm, which we reach through a gate. Turning immediately right, pass the gable-end of the farmhouse, then left through a small gate into a field down to another gate into a plantation through which the path drops gradually into a valley. Entering another field, strike across to the gate in the right-hand corner, and then cross the bridge to climb the steep lane until it converges with one from Mount Pleasant Farm on the right hand.

Here a gate on the left leads into and crosses a field. Our path follows the fence dividing a wood on our left from the three successive fields on the right. After which we climb a stile to descend a steep bank to join the riverside path bringing us to Leadmill Bridge.

Turning left over the bridge, proceed forward if Hathersage is to be our destination, but otherwise cross over the bridge and proceed down the old road on the right.

Turning right by the side of a building, follow the riverside to reach Harper Lees Farm on the left where the path steers across a large field and is walled along our left where it rejoins the river. Crossing another field, enter the wood, but soon branch left from the riverside path to climb up an old packhorse track, keeping left to the top corner of the wood. Crossing the railway bridge, the walls soon narrow to a gap and then fan out into National Trust property. Follow the wall to the rough road, then turn right. This leads over the old Bole Hill quarry cutting.

Here we turn left to cross left to examine the exposed foundations of Padley Hall with the restored Roman Catholic Chapel on the right. Then resume by the road to Grindleford Station.

There is a station at Hathersage on the Sheffield-Chinley L.M.R. line. There are also bus services to Manchester, Sheffield and Bakewell.

23

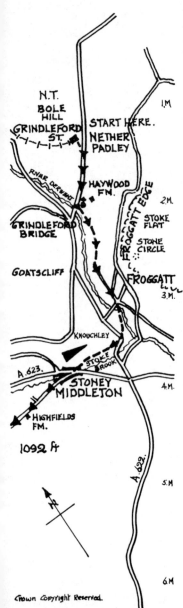

Grindleford Station, Froggatt, Stoney Middleton, Monsal Head

THIS walk links the Derwent and Wye and mirrors the changing moods of river and ravine and the moorland and mountain. We visit Froggatt, which has been described as "poor, proud and pretty"; Stoney Middleton, with tepid springs, unusual church nave, and Corn Law Repeal cross; Longstone Edge with extensive views; Great Longstone Church and Hall, and secluded Little Longstone, with its stocks and ancient manor house.

Leaving Grindleford Station by the main approach, join the road leading down past the Maynard Arms Hotel to the bottom of the hill, and pass St. Helen's Church (erected 1909) on the left and the restored toll-cottage on the opposite side near the bridge. Pass into the field on the left by a stile and follow the well-worn path over a stream and along the wall-side of a smaller field into Hay Woods, part of which has been cleared of timber to some extent. This is National Trust property.

The path continues across three fields and enters an occupation lane which leads into Froggatt. Across the river to our right we may catch a glimpse of Stoke Hall among the trees.

Continuing straight through Froggatt, cross the bridge on the right and immediately strike left through the riverside field, branching diagonally right once through the next stile to reach another stile in the corner. This leads one along the side of a wall up to the main road, which we cross and continue up the lane to Knouchley Farm.

Passing the farmhouse on our left, we enter a field and within a distance of 25 yards or so take a left incline to a stile beneath a couple of hedgerow trees. The field beyond may be under plough or growing crops, so instead of attempting to pass through the stile turn downfield to the second of two adjacent field gates. At second gate go over stile and follow the track forward, with Stoke Brook in the valley bottom on your left. Soon we are skirting the boundary wall to Stoney Middleton Hall, with the village cemetery on the right.

A stile admits to a lane where we notice a small stone trough on our right beyond two houses. This is fed by a warm spring which

24

also supplied the ruined "Roman" baths nearby. Turning sharply to the left we see St. Martin's Church (15th-century tower and curious octagonal nave built in 1759), then sharp right and left past the Post Office, crossing the main road to climb the steep road to the left of the cross erected in 1846 to celebrate the repeal of the Corn Laws.

The road continues uphill for a little over a mile (passing Highfields Farm) and then we turn left at cross-roads where an old lime kiln has caved in and continue along a rutted lane.

The lane dips steeply to cross a valley where it opens into moorland, but the path continues straight ahead. Continue over road and proceed through the small iron gates, keeping wall on left and then pass through three further gates. The path becomes lost among mining operations, but a stile can be seen straight ahead. Work to the right for a few yards and then swing left along a track into a tarmac road and follow this round the right-hand bend for a few yards. Then swing off the road on a left incline and drop down to a stile in 50 yards. Follow an indistinct path through a gorse thicket to the valley floor and cross the field.

Work on a right-hand incline round the bluff of outcropping rock for $\frac{1}{4}$ mile and then breast the slope to a stile in front in the stone wall coming down the right-hand hillside. The path then crosses a couple of fields and into a lane, from which we emerge to turn right to Great Longstone Church, with its "Welcome to hikers" sign. In the churchyard is a restored cross and the church itself has several interesting features, including a carved oak screen.

Leaving the churchyard by the "kissing-gate" in the right corner, we cross a small paddock into the main street opposite the village green, turn right past the gateway leading to the 18th-century Hall, then sharp left out of the village.

Soon we reach Little Longstone's string of houses, noticing the stocks in a recess on our right, and the picturesque manor house a little farther along on the same side. At the end of the hamlet is the little Congregational Chapel, and a short stretch of road brings us to our destination.

Route 11 can now be joined in Monsal Dale if it is desired to proceed further. Walking downstream will bring you into Ashford-in-the-Water in little more than an hour.

25

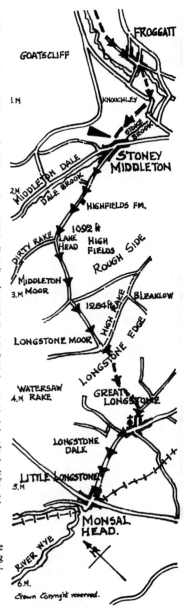

Crown Copyright reserved.

Wardlow Mires (or Tideswell), Monsal Dale, Ashford, Bakewell

FROM Wardlow Mires we pass through Wardlow and proceed down Ravensdale (where lilies of the valley grow) and join the Wye at Cressbrook Mill, for the rest of our journey through Monsal Dale to Ashford and Bakewell.

If desired, this walk may be started at Tideswell, in which case we turn left at the church gates, leaving the main road by Cliff Lane (which turns sharply right almost opposite the George Hotel) and proceed directly into Litton, passing the modern church and going straight through the village.

Leaving Peep o' Day House on the right (just over the hill) we carry on down the road for another 400 yards to a stile on the right, which takes us across three fields into the road at Wardlow Mires. On our right is St. Peter's Stone, a limestone crag which turns round each time it hears the cock crow! In a field beyond stood the gibbet of Anthony Lingard, who was executed for the murder of a tollkeeper.

From the Wardlow Mires take the Bakewell road into Wardlow to where it dips into a hollow just past the church. As the road beings to rise turn right up a narrow lane (signposted: Footpath to Ravensdale 1 mile). This is at the corner of a cottage. We continue forward into a grass-covered lane, until we reach a blank wall where another stile admits to the slopes of Ravensdale valley. Here the path veers left over the corner of the hill to drop steeply into the bottom. Cross the plank bridge, keeping left alongside the wall, with great crags towering above on our left. We soon reach Ravensdale (locally "Bury-me-wick") Cottages on our left.

As it climbs the hillside, the road improves and soon joins another, which is followed down to our left—to the bottom of the hill—with Bright Pool on the left and the mill on our right.

The road now runs parallel with the river and railway. Proceed past the road crossing to where it begins to rise steeply to Monsal Head. Here we leave the road to turn right through a gate by farm buildings and cross the footbridge and turn left by the path under the railway viaduct.

26

Climbing the stile by the right-hand gate, the path runs parallel with the wall and along the river bank past the weir, curving with the river as it winds round the foot of Fin Cop. Keep to the footpath on the right bank. We soon reach the Quaker Fishponds on our left, crossing a stream by a step stile past a public footpath notice, and up a narrow field to join the Taddington Dale road.

Turn left down the main road, noting a large block of limestone in the river where it runs close to the road. This is Warren Stone — a reminder of Hulac Warren, a notorious robber.

Another ½ mile farther along we leave the road by a small gate on our right, just before reaching a bridge beneath which the river flows, but not without noticing the outcrop of igneous rock at the corner round which the road disappears. Enter the gate — with its misleading "Fishing strictly private" notice — and follow the public footpath threading between the river and breeding ponds where rainbow trout are reared.

Directly opposite the road (A6) is White Lodge picnic area. Go through this to a marked and numbered stile way. Follow the path marked "No. 3" all the way to Ashford through Great Shacklow Wood, passing an old bobbin mill with latticed windows and twin water-wheels. Proceed through a stile to cross three more fields, before reaching the Sheldon road by a step-stile. Follow the road to the left, noting the derelict mill across a bridge where Ashford marble was once sawn and polished for inlaying.

We next join the by-pass road for a short distance, crossing over to turn left over Sheepwash Bridge and past the tithe-barn (now an art gallery) to the church.

Continue down the street, turn right at the Devonshire Arms, pass the Post Office and proceed along a stretch of road to cross a bridge mysteriously inscribed "M. Hyde 1664", over another bridge, and through a gate (signposted) on our left into a large meadow. This is crossed to rejoin the river, until near the weir, the path crosses a swampy valley and climbs a slight rise.

Proceed through five small fields and cut across Lakeside Estate and one more field to join the main road which is followed (left) into Bakewell.

Bus services connect Tideswell with Buxton, Sheffield, Chesterfield, Bakewell and intermediate places. Bakewell is the venue for buses for Derby, Matlock, Buxton, Chesterfield.

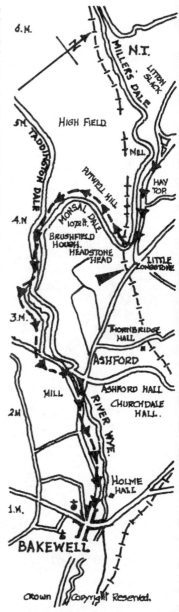

27

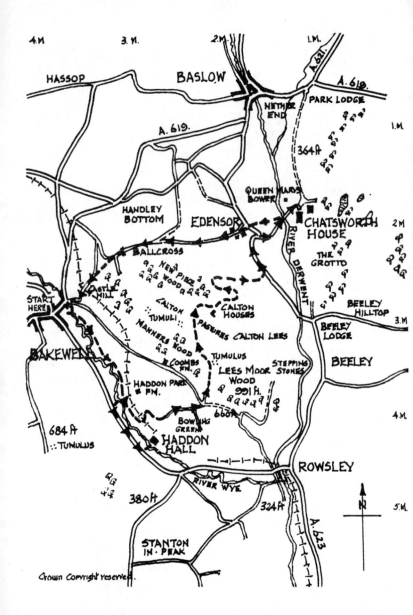

28

Bakewell, Haddon Hall, Chatsworth House, Edensor, Ball Cross, Bakewell

STARTING and finishing at Bakewell, the circuitous route takes us from the Wye to the Derwent, calling at Haddon Hall and Chatsworth House. We pass the Bowling Green above Haddon, the Russian Cottage on the edge of Chatsworth Park, and return from Chatsworth via the model village of Edensor.

Leaving Bakewell Square, proceed to the bridge and branch right along the promenade on the right bank of the river, crossing the concrete bridge about 100 yards farther along. Pass the timber yard and cross another bridge where we turn right to proceed past the showground offices of Bakewell Agricultural Society. Continue downfield along the track (with the show ring over the hedge on our left) to the stile ahead.

Follow the path along the left side of three further fields, before striking diagonally across the dark green streak of path with the "winding Wye" on our right. We soon cross a footbridge over a small stream and follow a well-defined path until the river takes a wide sweep away to the right. We now make straight for the opposite stile and gate in Haddon Park Lane, keeping to the slopes on our left in wet weather to avoid the intervening marshy ground.

(For the benefit of those not visiting Haddon Hall, it might be mentioned that we shall retrace our steps to this point, and the route up the lane will be resumed later).

Crossing the lane to the iron stile in the railings, the path becomes hemmed in by the river and railings and soon we catch our first glimpse of Haddon before crossing an ornamental concrete bridge, with the path fenced until we join the Bakewell-Rowsley road. Turning left along the beech hedge, we notice the milestone across the road informing us that London is exactly 150 miles away, and shortly turn left through the gatehouse arch and across the bridge to the Hall. (Not open Sundays or Mondays, except at Bank Holiday weekends).

Returning to the stile leading into Haddon Park Lane, we turn right and climb the winding road which turns left over the mouth of a disused railway tunnel, and soon see a notice on our right indicating "Public bridle road". The word "road" is something of a misnomer, for it has been partly obliterated. Entering the narrow gate, follow the railings on the right and pass through four more gates before reaching the ornate 18th-century Bowling Green, with stout walls and iron gates approached by a broad stone staircase with ball-topped balustrade.

As it continues by the side of the Bowling Green wall, the track more properly assumes the description of bridle road, climbing steadily to bear right with trees on the left and pastures on the right. When the road divides, we keep left across a valley which shelves away towards Bakewell on our left, and soon cross the old Rowsley-Bakewell road, at which point we are confronted by two gates.

Enter the gate on the left leading into Manners Wood. The track ascends steeply, soon affording a glimpse of a reservoir through the trees below. We eventually join another well-defined track which is followed for 100 yards before striking up to the right again. Proceed forward across several lateral paths to where our ascending track is skirted by a stone wall.

The way continues between banks of bracken and a wall, soon reaching a gap in the wall on our right at a magnificent viewpoint. Pass through gap and turn half left and cross through a plantation of young conifers. Make for a gate in a boundary wall at about 350 yards, but turn sharp right 12 yards short of the gate and proceed along boundary wall and over a ladder-stile into Calton Pastures.

Proceed downfield on a 45 degree left incline, dipping down between two stone water troughs in a hollow (unsighted until on top of them) and continue downfield to a natural gap in a gully and through a gate (about 300 yards on the left of Calton Houses). The path now mounts obliquely to the right and joins a broad grassy road on the top, which we follow a short distance to the right until we see a gate (the second gate, not the first) away on our left. This is about 300 yards to the left of Russian Cottage — a replica of a Russian-style house built of timber with elaborately decorated eaves, gables and shutters.

Entering the gate, we pass between a coniferous plantation on our left and a sycamore plantation to the right, and soon descend a wall-enclosed lane curving left to give access by a gate into Chatsworth Park and opening up a superb view of the woods, gardens and great house. It should be understood that the public are admitted to this particular area of the Park by kind permission of the Trustees of the Chatsworth Settlement.

We now make our way in a direct line across the Park towards the spire of Edensor Church, descending into a hollow in which is a small area of enclosed timber. Skirting the railings of this enclosure, we turn immediately right and follow the green track which soon swings left to join the main road. Continue along the road as it curves right to Chatsworth House itself. (Check for times of opening.)

Returning across the bridge, leave the road and take the path climbing up the hillside to the right over the shoulder of the hill to Edensor, the model village in which all the houses differ in architectural style.

Pass the modern church occupying the side of one destroyed by fire, and follow the road until the houses narrow to what appears to have been a toll-cottage on our right, when the lane deteriorates until we join the metalled road from Pilsley.

Continue to climb steeply with a mature plantation cresting the hill and an adolescent one farther along on the same side. Topping the hill, descend to where the road turns steeply right past Ball Cross Farm. If we have time for a short diversion, the lane to our left brings us to the grass-covered mounds of an Iron Age fort.

Retracing our steps from the fort, our path leads into the wood opposite the farm. Descend through the trees until a stile leads into the golf-course, cross to the stile at the bottom and renew acquaintance with the road just above Bakewell's now disused railway station. Continue down the road, until we reach the bridge from where we began our journey.

Bakewell is a centre for bus routes for Buxton, Sheffield, Derby, Chester-field and other places.

Fox House Inn, Froggatt Edge, Curbar, Backstone Edge, Baslow

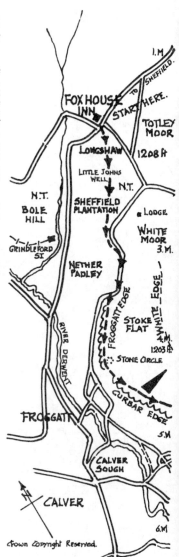

ALTHOUGH it departs in places from the mathematical definition of a straight line, this walk presents a succession of charming views and vistas. Starting at Fox House (the Whitcross of *Jane Eyre*), we pass Longshaw Lodge (former shooting-box of the Dukes of Rutland), and traverse once private coach-drives over rugged moorland and along escarpments fringing the Derwent. Landmarks include a stone circle, weird rock formations, Curbar Round House and Plague graves, Eagle Stone and the Wellington Monument.

Directly opposite the Fox House Inn is an entrance to the Longshaw Estate (N.T.) which leads to the main drive at the lodge cottage. Note the National Trust sign. Continuing down the drive, flanked by small stone monoliths, we leave it as it curves left and descend the steps (signposted) into a path across the front of Longshaw Lodge, with a sweeping moorland view to our right.

Passing through two wooden gates, we follow the grass-covered drive, noting the lake to our right. Having passed between two isolated gate stoops, the trees thicken into a wood and we soon pass through a stile near a gate intersecting the drive, and see a splendid view across fields to our right over the Derwent Valley. The road shortly snakes through a scattering of trees to join the busy main road where, turning right, we proceed down in the direction of Froggatt, passing the lonely Grouse Inn on the right hand side.

The road descends for several hundred yards before turning sharply right, where we see Stoke Flat reservoir on our left. We enter a small gate just below the reservoir on the left to follow the moorland track as it curves left over the shoulder of the hill to run roughly parallel with the escarpment of Froggatt Edge. Here and there are great outcrops of rock perched perilously on the very edge of the rocks. Shortly after crossing a stream and pass through a gate, we see a small circle of stones a few yards to the left of the track.

31

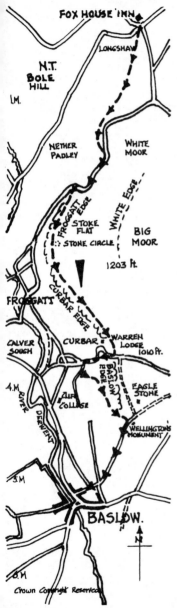

A little farther along, the road has been cut through several great crags weathered into fantastic shapes, one of which is known—when viewed from below—as the Batch of Oatcakes. Another is pocked with a series of indentations resembling "cup-marks", while several are pitted with "rock-basins" caused by erosion, and one imagines that these strangely impressive formations were once worshipped as rock idols. Sometimes there are fascinating views of the valley and distant hills framed by these rugged outcrops.

From the highest point of these crag-strewn moors, the track descends to Curbar Gap by a step-stile, from which point we can see an ancient guide stone in a field across to the left. We have two alternatives here. We can either cross the Gap directly on to Baslow Edge or follow the road down to the right towards Curbar. We then enter a stile on the lower side of the road to cross six small fields to rejoin the road shortly before entering the village.

After passing the first few houses, we turn left down a grassy lane, through a stile and past the curious Round House—so named because of its conical stone roof—where we again turn left through a stile and by a path leading diagonally up the field to enter rough moorland.

Our path joins a more prominent one leading to the right at a point near where there are five irregular stones in a slight depression. These are inscribed with initials and the date 1632, and identify the graves of the Cundys, who died of bubonic plague. Proceeding along the level track, we pass a stone structure reminding us that this is the Derwent Valley pipeline which we follow through an iron gate before branching up the rutted track to our left, ascending to the corner of a field which forms a boundary to the moors.

The path turns right, running parallel with the fence until entering a disused quarry which is crossed by a path to our left, again turning left up the old cart track to where paths divide to the Eagle Stone (on our left) and the Wellington Monument—at the edge of the escarpment of Backstone Edge. This name is derived from the fact that bakestones were once quarried here, but meddling surveyors thought the name an error and inserted "l" to make it Blackstone Edge.

32

Some writers say Eagle Stone is a corruption of Aigle Stone, named in honour of a Saxon deity who could throw stones which humans couldn't move. Baslow youths used to prove their courage and claim the hands of their sweethearts by scaling this landmark. The Monument was erected in 1866 to mark an earlier visit to the spot by the Iron Duke when staying as guest of the Duke of Rutland.

We retrace our steps to the disused quarry, joining a deeply fretted cart-track, which, passing through a gate, descends to Baslow. Where this track turns sharply left, we may take a short cut down through the trees to rejoin the road at the entrance of the township. Some of the houses on our left are built in the grounds of a former hydro, an establishment which prospered in the days when royalty frequently visited Chatsworth House. The road divides at the triangle and we have the choice of one to the left leading to the Nether End, and the other proceeding down to the Church.

Fox House Inn is served by buses operating from Sheffield, Castleton, Baslow, Bakewell and Chesterfield. Baslow, too, is similarly serviced for the journey home at the end of the walk.

BETTER FEEL SAFE THAN SORRY

FAR TOO MANY young people anxious to savour outdoor pursuits are venturing abroad ill-equipped for what may lie ahead. Miles of rough terrain to be found in and around the High Peak district is not "easy" walking country, for the weather can be a potent and cruel hazard when exploring these breathtaking uplands if one is not adequately equipped to meet the unexpected.

Top quality protective outer garments and stout footwear, as well as a rucksack containing adequate rations, a first-aid outfit, spare woollies, maps and compass, are essential if one is to avoid taking undue risks. These are minimum requirements for a single day's outing and will, of course, need to be augmented before setting off should the expedition be planned as an extensive walking tour in Derbyshire. It is much better to be prepared for any eventuality than to be caught out ill-prepared for the buffetings of fate in the shape of either foul weather or unfortunate mishap.

TRAVEL FACILITIES

PUBLIC TRANSPORT, both in regard to rail and bus services, has progressively contracted in recent years in some of the more remote areas of the Peak District. Consequently, ramblers have found it increasingly difficult to get to or from their favourite walking country unless they had their own means of transport.

To alleviate the situation a Peak Pathfinder bus service covering a network of routes between Ashbourne and Buxton and traversing Dovedale and the Manifold Valley areas with connections linking the Tissington Trail, is now operating on Sundays.

A timetable of bus routes feeding the Peak District National Park, including details of the Pathfinder service, is now available from the National Park office, Bakewell, or at English Tourist Board offices.

Baslow, Calver Sough, Coomb's Dale, Bakewell

FOR a short distance our route follows the Derwent, then passes through Calver (the Blossomby of Rev. James Cocker's *Blossomby Idylls*) and Calver Sough (so named from the "sough" driven to relieve local leadmines of water), up Coomb's Dale, noted for its lilies of the valley, and over two "rakes" where surface lead veins were once worked. The walk affords a variety of river, hill and valley scenery.

Leaving Baslow Church and crossing the old bridge with its quaint stone watch-box, turn right and proceed through Bubnell until the road dips past a wood on the left. At the bottom of the dip turn right through a stile and then turn half-left to cross the field to trees in front, where a track runs parallel with the river on the right-hand.

Very muddy in wet weather, the path leads into a wood and emerges near the riverside into a field. Cross the field on a left incline to another field. A step-ladder stile over a wall gives access to a narrow lane, which we cross to another field, bounded on the right by recent housing development. We emerge in Calver just below the Methodist Chapel.

Turning left up the street, branch right at the cross-roads (site of old cross now has a street lamp addition). Notice garden ornament of a salvaged window from Baslow's old toll house. Bear left. This is Lydgate, recalling times when men armed with watchbills kept their nightly vigil.

Keeping straight ahead to Calver Sough, cross over the main road to the road which leads to Stoney Middleton. We soon see a Highways Depot on our right. A little farther along, branch left up a lane to the right of which stands a small parish boundary stone.

The road winds through a valley for a mile or so until a neighbouring valley forks left, and here we take the path climbing steeply up the left-hand side of the main valley. There are magnificent views of Coomb's Dale and the sweeping ranges to the north-east as one steadily climbs the hillside. The going can be quite punishing at times, but taking the hillside in easy stages is the best antidote for this.

Reaching the top, we cross a field to an iron gate and an opencast site where barytes and fluor spar mining have obliterated the original path, but we go forward and make a slight detour (left) to reach the opposite gate. At this point we note the limestone walls of the worked out "rake" which runs in the usual east to west direction.

The gate leads through a field and farmyard where we see a good example of the limestone pitched mere for conserving water.

A stile admits to the next field and we proceed forward downfield to another mere. The path swings right and into another "rake" with disturbed contours. The route continues on a right incline over rough ground to a stile over a stone wall. We are immediately faced with another stile through a wire fence, which we ignore to turn left to a stile at the side of a gate and here we enter a bridle road. Proceed forward for 75 yards to a damaged footpath direction sign and continue down the bridle track to the road at the bottom, where we turn right to pass through the hamlet of Rowland. Joining the Hassop-Longstone road, cross on a slight left incline to the lane skirting Hassop Park. We then proceed through five fields with the path hugging the limestone wall. Then strike off to the right by a wire fence until the road is reached by a stile about 50 yards to the right of a toll bar cottage.

Turning left to the cottage, where we notice the bell and gate above the upstairs window in the gable, enter the field opposite by the gate and go forward to the level-crossing. Crossing the disused railway track, we breast the grass-covered lane mounting the hillside. The way is intersected by three gates and opens into an exceptionally large field. Continue along the wall on the left and past three wind-bent trees to enter another grass-covered lane, which soon begins to descend steeply. A panorama of Bakewell, in which the church steeple is dominant, opens up.

Pass through two more gates, and the lane soon opens into a field through the centre of which the path leads to a stile and gate at the bottom. Turn left through a wood, past the concealed chert quarries and equally well-concealed historic Holme Hall (of which we get a glimpse over its high wall) and then cross the River Wye by a paved packhorse bridge.

Notice the triangular quoins built for the convenience of pedestrians to avoid the bulky loads of the pack mules. Turning left, join the busy road from Buxton and proceed into Bakewell.

35

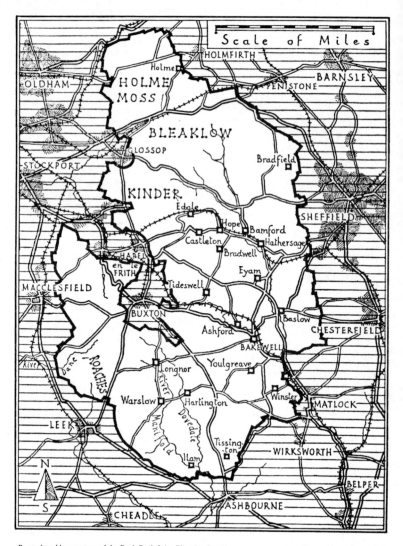

Reproduced by courtesy of the Peak Park Joint Planning Board

Crown copyright received

THE PEAK DISTRICT NATIONAL PARK

Buxton, Cat and Fiddle, Axe Edge, Three Shire Heads

IN this area of "over the tops" there are innumerable rambling excursions available, bringing within range such well-known places as the Cat and Fiddle Inn (on the Macclesfield road) and Three Shire Heads.

Public transport covering the area of Axe Edge is available from Buxton, Leed and Macclesfield.

Starting from Buxton, move off along St. John's Road (A53) and proceed for ¼ mile, until faced with a fork in the road at church.

If it is intended to make for the Cat and Fiddle, then bear right at the junction along an old route over the moors, the lane eventually petering out to little more than rough track.

On the other hand, if the preference is for the eastern slopes of Axe Edge, continue along the main road and ignoe the turn right for the road to Macclesfield. Proceed forward along the Leek road and continue for about ½ mile beyond the railway level crossing. A grass-covered cart track is then seen on the right hand winding back over the Edge.

Take this route, for it eventually brings us out on the Macclesfield road. The Cat and Fiddle Inn is soon discernible nearly two miles away.

We are shortly confronted with a road junction—one bearing away to the right past the Inn and on to Macclesfield. The other, the Congleton road (A54)—the left arm—runs past Danebower Quarries and close to the area of Three Shire Heads. Some 300 yards along this left arm of the junction, however, there is a left turn into a moorland track which will take us back over the Edge to the Leek road.

It is well worthwhile to turn right along the Leek road and walk a further mile to discover the source of the Dove, which is to be found some 20 yards inside a field opposite Dove Head Farm.

Returning to the main road again, go forward in the same direction as we were proceeding when we left the road and turn right up a lane at about 200 yards distance. Another 1½ miles of walking brings us out at Three Shire Heads.

37

Buxton, Solomon's Temple, Dale Head, Dowel Dale, Longnor

STARTING from Buxton Market-place, we first visit Solomon's Temple, then see Diamond Hill as we pass through the Mines Research Establishment. Our descent into the Dove valley provides unusual views of the twin Chrome (locally pronounced "Kroom") and Parkhouse Hill, before we cross into Staffordshire. We then skirt Nab End to reach the little "market town" of Longnor.

From Buxton Town Hall, follow the High Street to the junction of several road, choosing to bear right up Green Lane until a by-lane opposite College Road is reached. The lane soon narrows to the right and left, when we branch right up the steep footpath into a wood. Leaving the wood, our path continues up several small fields to reach the tower, which was built by a publican named Solomon. It contains a circular stone staircase with a handrail which enables us to reach the platform at the top, from where there is a sweeping view in all directions.

Leaving the Temple we continue forward, for the path descends a rocky slope to a stile which brings us into the Burbage-Harpur Hill road. Turn left and follow the road, which soon dips into Brookbottom, and then take the first turn right up a winding road, passing limeworks to the left and waste heaps on the right.

Across the valley to our right is Countess Cliff, which was formerly renowned as Diamond Hill because of the crystal prisms which are sometimes washed to the surface after a shower of rain. These appear to be in the limestone subsoils beneath the turf, and specimens were once prized by geologists.

The road curves to the right, passing mushroom culture nurseries on our left, and then turns leftwards over a bridge crossing a disused railway track. In front is the gateway entrance to the Mines Research Establishment. Enter and turn right (signposted: to Brandside) and proceed across the front of the Mines Research Establishment buildings. Continue forward and follow the road as it dips on a left-hand curve to a red-brick building. At the end of this

38

building turn right across some narrow-gauge railway tracks and follow a concreted roadway bearing left, parallel with the disused railway embankment on the right-hand.

This road soon dips into a valley to pass between the last of the scattered Research Establishment buildings. a signpost on another red-brick building at the far end ("Footpath to Brandside") indicates the route. The sign is again repeated 20 yards farther on to indicate a turn right across a lane to a stile leading into a field. Continue forward and upfield (with the old railway embankment swinging away on the right-hand) and cross over another disused railway track coming across from the left. There is an embankment and cutting on the right-hand as we cross over this old track.

The route continues straight ahead for a few yards and then takes a slight left incline across two more fields to the lonely Dale Head Farm, where we emerge into a roadway.

Follow the road to the left and over the brow of the hill. We soon begin to descend to cross a shallow valley before ascending the opposite hillside. Where we pass over a gated cattle-grid take the right-hand lane at the fork in the roadway and continue straight ahead through another gated cattle-grid on the crest of the slope. The serrated outline of Chrome Hill is in front.

The road now descends past Greensides Farm among the trees to enter Dowel Dale, at the entrance to which we pass a deep chasm in an enclosure to our left known as Owl Hole.

As we follow the valley its sides grow steeper, until they suddenly fall away when passing Dowel Farm, among the trees on our left. At the opposite side of the road a tributary of the Dove gushes out of a limestone cleft.

The valley through which we now pass is sheltered by Chrome Hill (access to which is gained by climbing a stile on the right ¼ mile further on) and Parkhouse Hill across on our left. Leaving the valley we soon see a footpath signpost indicating three routes. Follow the one pointing downfield to Longnor and cross the footbridge over the Dove into Staffordshire. The path climbs uphill on a left incline. We pass through a thin row of hedgeside trees to a stile on the top side of a walled enclosure to a farmhouse. We soon enter a lane which brings us to the main road, where we turn right for a mile walk into Longnor.

39

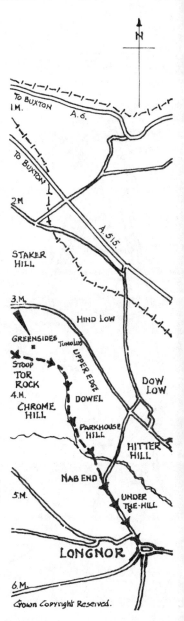

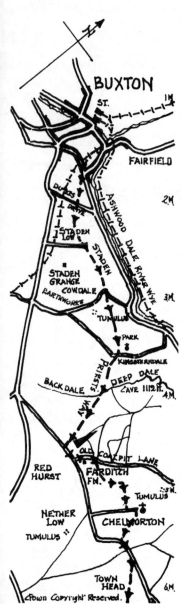

Route 17   8¼ miles
Buxton, Cowdale, Priest's Way, Chelmorton, Flagg, Monyash

THIS route passes beneath Staden Low, through Cowdale to Kingsterndale Church, and over Priest's Way into Deep Dale, site of Thirst House (a cave which has yielded rich archaeological treasures). Calling at Chelmorton and Flagg, where the High Peak Hunt point-to-point races are held annually, we reach Monyash, a former centre of the lead mining industry.

Leaving Buxton Town Hall, proceed through the market place along High Street, and turn left down Dale Road. Passing under the railway bridge, we drop down to take the right turn along Duke's Drive opposite the gas works. About 100 yards along on the right is a stile at the side of second field gate. We step through and traverse three fields and descend into the other leg of the loop of Duke's Drive. Enter the gateway on the other side and proceed forward up the lane and past farm buildings, then turn on a left incline up a grassy lane. Go forward with the wallside on the left and tree-crowned Staden Low on the right.

We soon reach the hamlet of Staden, so proceed forward over the miniature road junction and cross the front of two stone-built dwellings. In a matter of 75 yards we step inside the angle of a drystone wall on the right by means of a step stile barely discernible, so tumbled down is the wall hereabouts. Proceed downfield with the wall on the left-hand and continue forward, where a wire boundary fence is the left-hand marker, into Cowdale hamlet.

Turn right for a short distance and cross left-hand to a stile into a field and pass through the farmyard and along the left-hand wall of another field to enter a much larger field. Cross to the left-hand, distant, corner, for the path runs along the wallside and parallel with one on the other side which skirts the lovely wooded ravine of Kitty Dale. Then climb a step-stile into Kingsterndale Park and turn right-hand to follow the wire fence to the roadway. The village church is away on the left.

We now turn right for a short distance, crossing the road where it bends right. We enter a short lane into a large field, which is crossed diagonally to a pond at the junction with other fields. We are now on Priest's Way. At

40

the pond turn left through a fence and through the gate in a wall and proceed downfield by the left-hand wall until reaching a small gate. Step through and follow the path on a diagonal incline down the hillside. We reach the junction of three dales—Deep Dale, Back Dale and Horseshoe Dale. Proceed forward up Horseshoe Dale and out to the road, ¼ mile away.

Turn left and left again into Old Coalpit Lane (signposted to Taddington). On descending into an S bend enter the much-overgrown by-lane on the right. At an outlying farm building turn sharp left up the wallside and out by a gate into a rough lane. Turn right, then left, and follow the lane to a metalled road, where we turn right into Chelmorton.

Turning left by the school, we continue up the road to branch right just below the church. The road climbs along the hillside to unite with another road. Proceed forward to cross a transverse road to a stile (signposted to Flagg) a little farther along on the right.

The path crosses the field diagonally on a left incline to a stile in a broken down wall. Proceed forward with a boundary wall on the left-hand to a solitary chestnut tree shading a step-stile into the next field. Cross the centre of the field and through shallow mining outcrop and then veer left uphill to a gap in another boundary wall.

Continue forward with a boundary wall on the right to a stile under trees near a farmyard and proceed uphill to the roadway. Turn right and, ignoring the first lane opening, swing left into Flagg.

A stile on the right (signposted to Hurdlow Town) is entered and we cross a field to another stile which leads us through two further fields to a stile on the right of some dwellings. We turn right on to the road and immediately left until the road swings right. Here we proceed forward into the farm road to Knotlow Farm. The road swings right past the farm buildings and we go forward to the top left corner. A stile gives access to a grassy lane which divides at a triangle near a barn. Keep along the lane on the right until reaching a stile on the left just short of the first farm.

Taking the path through six small fields and an occupation lane to a stile by the gable-end of a cottage, we soon enter Monyash—journey's end.

Monyash is a convenient starting point for an extended tour of Lathkill Dale. *See pages 42 and 43.*

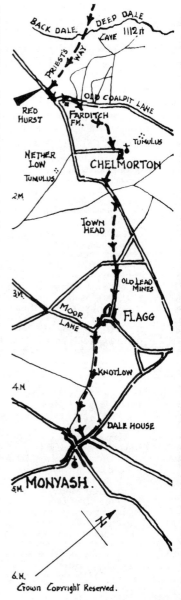

41

Monyash, Lathkill Dale, Alport

With alternative routes from Arbor Low and Haddon Hall

THERE are several points of access into Lathkill Dale, where the crystal clear stream is a delight to anglers and walkers alike, but as our previous walk finished at Monyash, we may as well use this former lead-mining centre of the High Peak as our starting point for the north-western approach into this most fascinating of Derbyshire dales.

Less than ½ mile to the east of Monyash, at the bottom of the dip on the Bakewell road (and within sight of the outskirts of the village) there is a field gate leading off southwards downfield into Lathkill Dale.

Proceed down the field, and where a choice lies between continuing along the cart-road ascending the higher ground on the right to One Ash Grange or proceeding down the defile on the left, then follow the latter route. Do not be put off by the waste dumpings of the old Ricklow Quarry, for the effort is well rewarded later on. The going is still somewhat rough when we reach the visible source of the River Lathkill in a low-roofed cave at the base of the hillside on the right.

After another ½ mile the main stream is joined by another emerging from Cales Dale on the right.

Continuing down the left bank, we readily notice the abundance of trout in sunlit pools on entering the woodlands near the middle reaches of the Lathkill. At the mill farther on a narrow lane climbs the hillside to Over Haddon, where we may enjoy a pleasant diversion to the village, or continue downstream and soon discern the stone buildings of the village on the high ground to the north.

Farther downstream from Over Haddon we cross the river by Conksbury Bridge. We may then proceed through the fields to Alport (another ¾ mile) by first ascending the road to Youlgreave for some 200 yards before mounting a stile on the left and joining a field path which eventually brings us closer to the river again near Raper Lodge. Continue down the path to Alport, where buses to Bakewell or Matlock may be joined.

Arbor Low and Cales Dale

An alternative route into Lathkill Dale, incorporating a visit to Arbor Low, an ancient stone circle, is to walk from Monyash along the road to Parsley Hay for nearly two miles, turning left up Long Rake at a point some 300 yards before reaching the junction with the main Ashbourne-Buxton road.

We proceed up Long Rake and over the brow of the hill—passing a plantation on the right—until we reach a field gate on the right leading to a farm. Turn in here for Arbor Low—beyond the farmhouse.

Returning to Long Rake, turn right for Youlgreave. Within ½ mile a cow-grid entrance to a farm road on the left (which swings downfield past Cales Farm) leads to One Ash Grange, where we turn at right angles to drop into Cales Dale. Or, with permission from Cales Farm to cross their land, we may drop down immediately into the head of the dale. It is fairly rough travelling, especially in a wet season, and one needs a stout stick to force a way through innumerable nettles in summertime as well as to assist one over rough ground.

Eventually joining up with Lathkill Dale, we can take the choice of either proceeding upstream to Monyash or downstream to Over Haddon or Alport, following the route previously described.

Across Haddon Fields

A pleasant walk of some two miles following a visit to Haddon Hall (not open Sundays or Mondays, except at Bank Holiday weekends) is obtained by crossing the Matlock-Bakewell road from the entrance lodge to Haddon and following a track to be found on the Bakewell end of the car park. Proceed through open fields after climbing the gently sloping hillside.

The path is a little indistinct hereabouts, but we should keep parallel with the boundary wall on our left, moving slightly across to our right to negotiate a step-stile over an intervening wall.

At farm buildings sheltered by a plantation continue forward over a stile at the side of a wicket-gate. Make diagonally for fence on left hand and mount through stile halfway along it. Keep the fluor-spar mining operations on the left and work left-handed, then right, through the trees to drop down into Lathkill Dale.

At the packhorse bridge over the river, one may rest for a time to survey the crystal-clear waters, with trout lying handy just beneath the surface awaiting some tasty morsel on the wing which may come within striking distance.

After crossing the bridge we are faced with a solitary dwelling — Raper Lodge. We can either continue on past the Lodge to Youlgreave, or turn right upstream to Conksbury Bridge, or left downstream through the fields to Alport village.

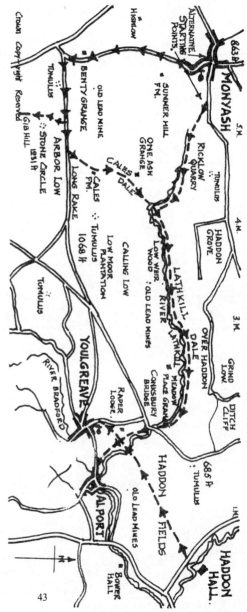

43

Matlock, Winster, Birchover, Stanton Moor, Rowsley

THIS walk takes one into high limestone country with its many hummocky fields as evidence of the activities of the old lead-miners, and on to the gritstone plateau of Stanton Moor, site of a prehistoric stone circle and of many prehistoric burial chambers. The Moor is of national archaeological importance (and excellent — although windy — for picnics).

From Matlock Bridge, bear right past Williams Deacon's Bank. A few yards farther on, to the left, is a footpath signed to Masson and Bonsall. Take it, striking straight uphill (not forking to the left) through a series of stiles and across two farm tracks. After the second track, with farm buildings at the left, the path goes through a gate stile to the far corner of the field, then straight along the wall to a lane. Twenty yards to the right down the lane, go through a stile in the wall on the left.

The path keeps to the right of a quarry. At a lane, go right for a few yards, then left again through a stile and straight on to a second, sunken, green lane. Turn left down this lane and continue into Bonsall Town Head. There, go right at old (Twigg) fountain, and up the hill to the right; then first left, and subsequently first right (by a letter-box). At the end of the houses, ignore the right turn and continue

44

straight down the lane, which becomes a track. At the beginning of a rise, the track forks.

At the junction of tracks, go left, then right. In $\frac{1}{4}$ mile, another lane comes in from the left. Go diagonally across the field between the two lanes, and head across the old lead mine workings to the road. Turn left.

A few yards farther on, take a path diagonally across the large field on the right. Beyond, stiles indicate the path to the high ground overlooking Wensley Dale, and it then drops down (to the right of a copse) into Winster.

Turn left, and walk through Winster. About $\frac{1}{4}$ mile past the church, turn right along a road marked "Unsuitable for motors" and rise to Upper Town (notice the stocks at the T-junction) and on to Birchover proper.

At Birchover turn right, and bear right (towards Stanton Lees) at the road junction $\frac{1}{4}$ mile ahead. After another $\frac{1}{4}$ mile, a sign indicates a track which goes up to the left to the Stanton Moor Stone Circle.

Follow the main track (not diverting to the right) straight up to the top of the moor, noting on the right (250 yards up) the laid-open Bronze Age burial chamber, and, on the left at the far end of the moor, the Nine Ladies' stone circle of the same period. The tower at the eastern edge of the Moor commemorates the 1832 Reform Act.

At the far end of the track across the moor, turn left on to the road, and then after 250 yards turn right on to a footpath which runs along the bottom edge of a wood, and so on to the road which goes to Pilhough and then Rowsley.

THE COUNTRY CODE

for visitors to the countryside

Guard against all risk of fire.

Fasten all gates.

Keep dogs under proper control.

Keep to the paths across farm land.

Avoid damaging fences, hedges and walls.

Leave no litter.

Safeguard water supplies.

Protect wild life, wild plants and trees.

Go carefully on country roads.

Respect the life of the countryside.

Matlock, Cocking Tor, Dethick, Riber, Matlock

THE interest of this route (a circuit east of Matlock) is primarily scenic, but Dethick (with its fine little church, and associations with Anthony Babington of the Babington Plot) is an optional extra. A close-up view of Riber Castle, built a century ago by John Smedley, is a fitting climax to our walk, during which this splendid eye-catcher is many times seen from a distance.

Leave Crown Square, Matlock, by the Alfreton road. Where, after ½ mile, the fields begin, take a footpath which leads off to the left between the Ernest Bailey Nursery and the Scout headquarters. Go along this path to the road at Lumsdale. Turn left here and follow the winding road uphill. Then, after a picturesquely derelict mill on the left, there is a sign to the right, marking a footpath to Tansley, via Oaksedge Lane.

Take this path. After rounding a pond, it becomes a rough track passing below some old quarries and commanding excellent views of the valley on the right and the high ground beyond. The track soon drops down towards Tansley, and is joined, near some cottages, by another track coming

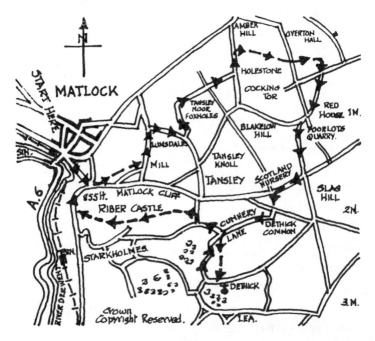

down from the left. Go up this, turn right at the top, and walk the length of the lane which goes for $\frac{1}{4}$ mile direct across Tansley Moor to a T-junction. Turn left there.

Four hundred yards up the road a stile to the right indicates a footpath leading through a spinney. Take this path. From the far end of the field beyond the spinney strike diagonally across the field towards a stile in the wall to the right of another spinney. The path goes diagonally across the next field again, to an up-and-over stile. Turn right towards the windpump, but about 70 yards short of it go through a stile and head towards another one through which the path goes towards some farm buildings and so out (to the left of them) on the road.

Turn right, and 100 yards down the road turn to the left through a stile, following a footpath which leads to the right of the Round Plantation, and on to the far right-hand corner of the field. Go through the next field, and to the rough land round the rocks of Cocking Tor on the right. In front, the ground falls away sharply and impressively.

Immediately below are the abandoned workings of an old lead mine. To the left, beyond the River Amber, is Ashover. In the distance to the right is the Ogston Reservoir, created by the damming of the Amber.

From Cocking Tor a path drops down to the right to a track below. Follow this to the right, between high banks. Carry straight on over the crossroads at the head of this track, and ignoring the right fork immediately adhead, go forward past the Poorlots Quarry, now a refuse dump on your right, and on to the next crossroads. Turn right here. On the left-hand side of the road, 300 yards down (opposite the far end of Scotland Nursery and below a new bungalow) notice an old guide-post (dated 1719) now used as a gate-post. Its sides are marked to point respectively to Wirksworth, Derby, Chesterfield and Bakewell, and it must have been brought here from elsewhere.

Take the next turning on the left, and at the end of the lane go across the main road into Cunnery Lane. Follow this for about $\frac{1}{4}$ mile until, just after passing Cunnery Wood on the left, a signpost on the left indicates the way to Dethick, Lea and Holloway. In this direction, if time allows, a worthwhile detour of rather under $1\frac{1}{4}$ miles can be made.

Take the bridle road to Dethick, then the first stile on your right and follow the wall to the right, turning left to subsequent stiles over the brow of the hill and straight down towards the turreted tower of Dethick Church. Turn right on to the road there.

The fine views to the left take in high ground beyond the Derwent valley. After going down the road 350 yards, turn right on to a bridle path back towards Tansley. In its upper part, the path is narrow, high-banked and leafy.

Rejoining the main route at the head of this path, turn left into Cunnery Lane. At the road, 400 yards ahead, turn right, and 250 yards down it take a signposted path to the left towards Riber. The path goes straight along the sides of fields until, after $\frac{1}{2}$ mile, a long field is reached, lying at right angles to the line of the path. Go diagonally across the corner of this field, and then straight ahead again until a track at the edge of Riber is reached. On reaching the road, strike to the right uphill towards the outbuilding of Riber Castle. Do call at the Wild Life reserve located there.

From the Castle, a well-defined footpath leads down to Matlock, reaching the road by passing to the left of the secondary school. Turn right, then just past the Parish Church turn left down a short steep hill, and left again into a park and the centre of Matlock.

Cross o' th' Hands, Kirk Ireton, Harboro Rocks, Matlock

THE walk, although almost entirely by road, has some fascinations in marked contrast to the Dethick walk (Route 22—*see pages 50 and 51*).

From the Cross o' th' Hands the road to Idridgehay drops sharply in a swinging S. At the second bend, what appears to be no more than an accommodation road turns off left between a spinney and a small brick farmhouse standing back in a field. The land soon begins to drop sharply to the little bridge over Sherbourne Brook. The hollow of the old way can easily be seen on the left of the lane for some distance down.

The lane saunters on, rather switchback fashion, but pleasantly enough from Ireton Wood to Kirk Ireton, where I hope the time is convenient for a call at the Barley Mow, the sort of inn where we wish we could tune ourselves into the radiations of several centuries of stories and gossip. The old church down the road is worth a visit, for there are distinct traces of Norman masonry.

Half a mile beyond, the road rises to Moorside, a most exposed spot four square to every wind that blows. As we crested every rise for miles back it stood up on the skyline. The gossip at the inn must have been of many a man who met his end at the crossroads here, where the gibbet stood. Where the road rises again through a deep hollow, a lane to Wirksworth turns off right, and a short way below in a hollow is Callow Hall Farm. The remains of a moat and an interesting 15th-century vaulted undercroft are here.

With Rough Pitty Side falling away steeply on the right the road plunges down to Hopton. At the bottom on the left a new farmhouse stands on the site of the queer and ruinous Stainsborough Hall. If your object is Wirksworth take the winding grass-grown Summer Lane going off right almost opposite Stainsborough Hall. It was an old drovers' way and is perhaps a pleasanter way and certainly less hilly than the road. At the junction with the Wirksworth-Ashbourne road look at the old signpost date 1709. Here are three ways but the post shows a fourth long since disused. It can be traced behind the farm and we shall pick it up a couple of miles away.

48

In contrast with the exposed road we have followed, the way left through Hopton to Carsington is very pleasant and sheltered.

If the weather is bad or misty, turn off right uphill in Hopton opposite the hall grounds. It is very pleasant and climbs over by Ibet Low. It actually marks the lost line of the old road we followed from Cross o' th' Hands. At the crossroads carry straight over under the old High Peak Railway bridge and past the industrial one on the left. At the fourth power cable pole past the red iron railings on the left a stile marks a wide diversion. This leads to a path up the hillside on to the old road again, here called Chariot Way. Turn right along this grass-grown road leading straight down to Grangemill.

The alternative route by Harboro Rocks is rough, has no defined path, and can be dangerous if the bearings cannot be seen. It is an old miners' path across an area riddled with old workings.

Carry on through Hopton to Carsington, and exactly where the road swings sharp left there is a jitty climbing steeply upwards on to the open hillside. Here bear half left as far as two low outcrop stones, then sharp right past a hawthorn tree to the line of power cable poles. Go parallel with these to the top of the rise.

Now aim midway between Harboro Rocks on the skyline and a pylon to the left, and keep this bearing until near the road. The easiest place to cross on to the road is at the cable pole bearing nearest to the rocks.

Follow the road towards the firebrick works, and before reaching the works a stile on the right leads on to a path giving access to the rocks. Fine views are to be seen on the top as far as the Wrekin and the Charnwood hills. This complex of rocks has yielded a great deal of evidence of prehistoric times.

From the summit aim easterly for a newly-made driveway leading to the works on the ridge. Be very careful about walls. Follow the road down to the Chariot Way already mentioned.

Cross straight over on the road towards Winster and then turn immediately right up the Salter's Way to Matlock. This again is another cross country trading track older than history. And so down the steep side of Masson, and if you care to turn right at the sharp lefthand twist at the bottom you will find the hollow of the road leading you straight to Matlock Bridge.

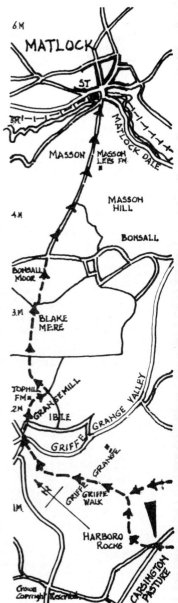

49

Ambergate, Shining Cliff Wood, Whatstandwell, Lea and Dethick, Bilberry Knoll, Cromford Canal

THE walk may easily be taken in parts, as the mood and weather dictate, and it is at most points readily accessible by bus. It abounds in tempting offshoots which may be explored later, and the scenery is varied and always charming, apart from minor blemishes through industrial development in the Derwent valley.

We start, then, at Ambergate Church where the road turns off the main Derby-Matlock road towards Shining Cliff Wood. Beyond the bridge over the Derwent and the mill stream, turn right at the first fork. At the top of the rise we again take the right fork down through the wire-works yard, which makes no pretence but of being just that. The site appears to have a continuous history as an iron forge from the days of the ancient royal forest of Duffield, of which these woods were part and we are following one of its ancient roads.

The works behind, our way lies through unspoiled woodlands with glimpses of the river below and, maybe, the cliff of Crich standing out almost like a miniature Matterhorn in the sunshine. At another fork in the track a ½ mile or so beyond the wire-works we take the left-hand track, which leads up through Alderwasley Park. A natural rock seat from which a magnificent view may be enjoyed offers a good place for a "breather". Alderwasley Hall is now a boys' school. On leaving the park follow the road round to the right. The old chapel, now rather sadly locked up and derelict, stands away on the hillside on our left. It is now a straight road and steady drop to Whatstandwell.

Cross over the bridge and walk up the road to Crich for a few yards then turn sharp left (after crossing the canal) along the lane to Holloway. The lane, overhung with trees, rises steadily. Where the road dips into a bend to the hamlet of Robin Hood (at a point about 100 yards *before* reaching the road bridge over a stream) a path runs off right into the woods near an old lamp-post. Continue forward through the old quarries, now overgrown with fern, silver birch and mountain ash. Higher up the track we cross a tumbling stream and carry forward, ignoring a stile on our left, with the stream on our right.

Emerging through the third stile at the end of the woods and into a field, proceed forward as though making for Crich Stand on the cliff in front. When about 150 yards inside the field bear leftwards, with the boulder-strewn hedge (and stream) on the right hand. Carry forward along this boundary line to the road in front, where we emerge through a stile with a signpost pointing in the opposite direction to Robin Hood.

Turn left along the Crich-Holloway road and proceed forward for 150 yards before turning right along a farm track to Wakebridge Manor Farm. Our way follows a track rising up to the left of the farm. This is a medieval road leading straight to Dethick, but a little difficult to follow in two places. On the top the way leads directly to a field between two stone gate posts with a stile at the corner of a large field on the left. The path here is obliterated, but goes diagonally across the field, when the hollow of the track is seen between widespaced walls dropping to a road going to Holloway.

The stile across the road marks the path. If the field is cropped it is important to go straight ahead, aiming for a small tree. A stile into the field beyond will give you a bearing. A line of well-worn paved stones used to mark the way, but it is easily followed by the stiles. Within about a couple of fields from Lea the path bears left towards a section of broken wall. It is on the edge of a deep sunk medieval road, Town Lane, which is followed right for 30 yards until a stile high up on the left side marks the continuation of the path diagonally into the village of Lea.

Turn right to a footpath which descends to a stream in the deep tree-filled gully, crossed by a little stone bridge. Out at the top again Dethick Hall farm and the lovely little chapel of the Babingtons is away on our left.

The key to the chapel may be had at the farm behind. A gate in the wall round the corner is the way to it. The kitchen of the Hall farm is part of the original hall, and there are other remains. The country about here is quite unspoiled and lovely. It is well worth reading the history of the Manor.

Out on the road, turn down left as far as the T roads at the bottom of the hill. Turn left a few yards to look at two very charmingly situated houses. Our way, however, is to the right past Littlemore Wood. There is no right of way through the wood and the only direction that can be given is to follow this pleasant lane up towards Riber for ¼ mile and then turn off just above a bungalow (Littlemoor Cottage) on the left hand along the farm track on the left to the little hamlet of Hearthstone.

This lies alongside Hearthstone Lane along which we turn left towards Bilberry Knoll, and simply follow the lane — it is a grassgrown track — down to Castletop Farm. Here is an

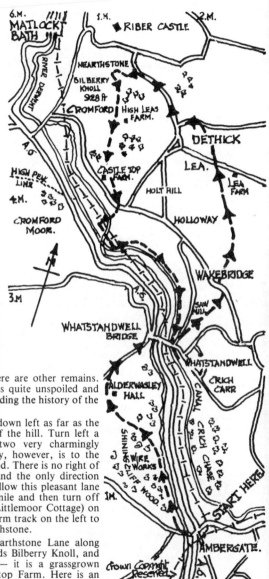

enchanting walk of lovely views, and there is rarely anyone about to enjoy them.

If it is so desired, you may take a footpath off right immediately due east of Cromford to which it will take you. The stile is where a belt of trees comes up to the lane. In wet weather the first part is almost impassable, however, and its direction is far from obvious.

At approximately 75 yards below Castletop Farm pass through the right of twin farm gates (on the left) along a track which proceeds, below a stone boundary wall, across the front of a cottage smallholding. The way leads through woodland to Lea Bridge. Where the track emerges on the main highway at Lea Bridge, turn right downhill for 150 yards and turn left between stone houses. Within 30 yards (once over a stream) turn immediately left along the side of the stream and behind another house and proceed up to the towpath of what was a branch of the Cromford Canal. Turn right-hand along the towpath and continue forward over the railway line at the mouth of Leawood Tunnel.

A little farther on we join the main canal and proceed over a foot-bridge to the other bank to turn left along the towpath to Whatstandwell, or even on to Ambergate. This stretch of canal makes a delightful end to the walk. The thrill of walking through the canal tunnel adds piquancy to this stretch.

You could have travelled much farther and then have found it difficult indeed to better this walk.

Route 23 6 miles

Morley, Stanley, Dale Abbey, Risley

SHALL we call this an odd walk? One of those for a spare afternoon when you want to do something out of the usual run of Derbyshire charms and felicities. It walks into a coalfield and out again on to a very main road, but it takes in a remarkable church, an abbey, a portway we could trail across the county, and what we may surmise to be a branch running down to the Trent at Sawley.

We could pick up our road sooner, but a gap now impossible to follow would mean a long deviation, so take the bus to Morley.

Our road dips sharply down right past Morley Church, which must be seen. In the spring the churchyard is a mass of daffodils. Much of the stained glass came from Dale Abbey and is a very fine example of medieval craftsmanship.

The modern road turns off right at the bottom of the hill. Carry straight on along the lane by the rectory. On the right you can see fishponds and probably the site of the manor mill. We pass an odd house here and there, and eventually the lane becomes grassgrown—and in wet weather extremely muddy.

Continue straight down to wicket-gate and follow hedge downfield to footbridge over brook. Follow path to further gate and road bridge straddling the now disused railway track. Continue to road and turn right at T into Stanley along Morley Lane.

And was it not in the village of Stanley, as the Chronicle of Thomas de Musca tell us, that the virtuous baker of Derby, looking for a place to make his hermitage heard a woman saying to a girl: "Take your calves with you: drive them as far as Deepdale and make haste back". Taking this as divine guidance the baker went with the girl and so found a hillside in which to carve his hermitage — which we will see.

We will follow in his footsteps. At the main road in Stanley go south (towards Derby) and take the first turn left beyond the brook (at Bridge Inn). This is Dale Road. The route is at first another reminder of coal, then continues first as a track under the high tension cables and at Hagg Farm as an accommodation road.

Beyond Hagg Farm turn right on the lane and go straight over the main Spondon-Ilkeston road down to Dale. On reaching the inn we turn right into the village, where you will see quite a number of relics of the abbey's domestic buildings.

Follow the lane as far as where the frame of the great east window stands forlorn on the left and turn right up the farm track to the little church-cum-house (once a public house). The key may be had here. The little church is indeed worth a visit. It was probably one of several original attempts to found the abbey and later on, perhaps, was the infirmary chapel of the abbey, although no-one is certain. There are some well-preserved medieval murals to be seen which are worthy of close scrutiny.

Continue behind the farm and through the yard left. A footpath leads along the slope of the hillside into a spinney. The hollow of the old road is seen on the left, and above on the right with a platform in front, where a penthouse stood, is the hermitage. Do read the story of the hermit and the founding of the abbey.

The path goes on into the field beyond where we veer right to the corner, where the road to Stanton — a continuation of our track — makes a T with the road from Dale to Sandiacre. Turn right up this road.

At Boyah Grange we follow the turn sharp left and continue forward for half-a-mile where an accommodation road goes off diagonally right at a spot where the main highway swings on a left incline. Follow the lane round to Park Farm and turn into a field on the left by the gate directly opposite the farm. Move downfield close to the hedge on the right and cross the stream in the dingle by the wooden bridge. From the stile beyond aim straight upfield to Risley Lodge Farm which you skirt on your left. You will then find yourself on a farmroad which leads downhill to Risley (opposite the Blue Ball Inn).

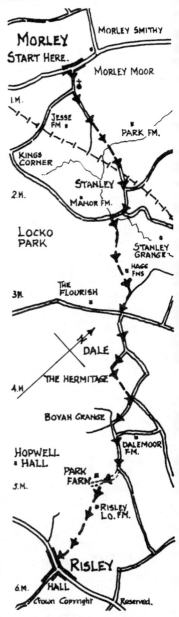

53

Ashbourne, Mapleton, Ilam, Manifold Valley, Hulme End

ASHBOURNE — the gateway to Dovedale and the Manifold Valley — is admirably situated for the start of a two-day circular tour of this renowned area of scenic beauty. Some of the finest walking country to be found anywhere in the British Isles is available here, a fact which is very much apparent at holidaytimes and on fine week-ends, when visitors crowd the lower reaches of the dales.

There are, however, plenty of wide open spaces to the north—sufficient for the most fastidious of individuals not to feel unduly hemmed in. But for obvious reasons, where there is a preference for solitude, midweek is the best time for exploration unhampered by the presence of others.

Starting from Ashbourne, then, strike off up the Buxton Road from the Market Square. About fifty yards beyond the Bowling Green Hotel (at the corner of North Avenue), where the main road begins to dip after coming over the brow from the centre of Ashbourne, there is a gate on the left-hand which leads into a field.

Enter the field and continue down the side of the hedge and over the Bentley Brook at the bottom. Proceed under the bridge and along the path which turns right to run parallel with the old railway track, now the grass-covered Tissington Trail for pony trekking and rambling, for a distance of about 100 yards. Then turn left through an opening in the fence and mount the slopes over the hillside.

Follow a course veering slightly to the right, but keep a sharp lookout for the stiles ahead in the hedgerows, as these are the only indication of the footpath in places. Eventually we are rewarded with some magnificent views across Okeover Park, with the village of Mapleton nestling at our feet.

Descend the hillside into the village and turn right when emerging on to the main road. Proceed as far as the road junction and turn left along the arm which leads to Okeover Hall for a distance of about 300 yards. At the approach to the bridge over the Dove there is a stile on the right which gives access to the river bank. Proceed upstream—still on the Derbyshire side, by the way—and continue in conjunction with the river winding its course

54

away on our left for a mile and a half until Coldwall Bridge is reached.

Do not cross over the bridge to the Staffordshire side of the river, but again proceed upstream on the east bank until reaching the outskirts of Thorpe Village — on the road to Ilam.

As we intend exploring the Manifold Valley, turn left over the bridge into Staffordshire and continue past the entrance to Dovedale and the Izaak Walton Hotel (on the right) and proceed forward along the road into Ilam.

Continue into the drive to Ilam Hall and follow the path through the grounds to the bank of the Manifold. Follow the path upstream for about ½ mile and then cross over the footbridge. A few yards along the path after crossing over the bridge turn right up the track leading to Throwley Hall. The river, during a wet season, at least, winds its way over on the right hand, parallel in some degree with the direction we are following.

Keep to the left of the ruined Hall and of Throwley Hall itself and cross over the road coming in from the left, and forward through the stiles towards a belt of trees and a step-stile. Once over the stile ignore the track coming in from the left. Now go down through the trees on a right incline to a gate in the bottom corner (signposted) and so to the valley where the river Hamps joins the Manifold (on our right) under the bluff of Beeston Tor.

Cross the Hamps and go forward (do not bear left) along a first-rate level footroad — formerly the track of the now defunct Manifold Valley Light Railway.

Further directions are hardly necessary, for this most exhilarating and pleasant footroad travels through magnificent valley scenery for a further five miles until one reaches the old railway terminus at Hulme End.

Interesting diversions can be made, however, to Wetton Mill and to Butterton.

There is no longer a bus service available at Hulme End to Buxton or Ashbourne so other independent arrangements have to be made for the return journey home.

Alternatively, a stay overnight in the area — either at Hulme End or Hartington (two miles away) — has one conveniently poised for the next stage of this circular tour: Dovedale, from north to south, described in *pages 56 and 57*.

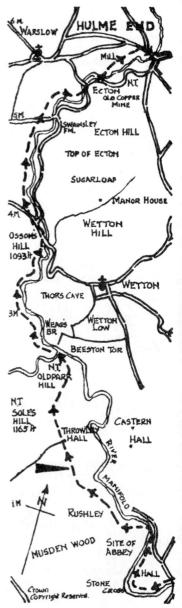

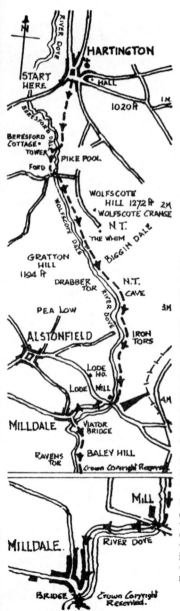

DOVEDALE
Hartington to Thorpe

MANY ramblers fail to realise that, so far as Dovedale is concerned, the beauties of the gorge are shared equally by both Staffordshire and Derbyshire—the latter county usually being ascribed a larger measure of the credit probably as a result of the footpath being situated on the Derbyshire bank of the river for most of its length between Beresford Dale and Thorpe Cloud.

The Manifold Valley—which also runs a parallel north to south course some two to three miles west of Dovedale—is entirely in Staffordshire, but both valleys are complementary to a limestone area of exceptional scenic beauty.

There are several points of access into Dovedale, the more popular route being the southern approach from Thorpe.

For the purpose of this ramble, however, the northern approach to Dovedale from Hartington is preferred—as a continuation of a circular tour from Ashbourne after having already explored the Manifold Valley in the preceding pages of this book.

We must first look for a stile at the side of a transport garage just round the corner from Hartington Post Office—along the road to Hulme End.

Entering the fields by way of the stile, bear right along a clearly indicated track, soon crossing over a rough cart-track running at right angles across the route. Continue through open fields for a short distance with a slight right incline, but head towards a tree-lined hillside in front—the bastion of Beresford Dale, which itself is the first of half-a-dozen dales to comprise the Dovedale area proper.

The River Dove is seen on the right, twisting its way across fields towards the neck of a narrow passage through overhanging rocks in front—the point we are making for.

Barely discernible through the trees on the far bank—and strictly private property—is the celebrated Fishing Temple (erected in 1674) which commemorates the association of Charles Cotton, of Beresford Hall, with Izaak Walton, whose exploits in the gentle art of fly-fishing are immortalised in the 17th-century classic, *The Compleat Angler*. It is a stone, single-roomed building with steeply-pitched roof.

As we cross the footbridge over the river we are at Pike's Pool, denoted by a monolithic finger of rock rising clear from the water to a height of about 30 ft.

Continuing downstream recross the river at the end of Beresford Lane and go forward across an open meadow into Wolfscote Dale.

Continue down the left bank of the river for a distance of 2½ miles as far as the Lode Mill, where a road bridge crosses the stream. Should the rambler feel disinclined to continue downstream, he or she can turn left on mounting the bridge from the riverside walk and breast a stiff climb up to the New Inns Hotel at Alsop-en-le-Dale (about ¼ mile away). *A regular bus service is no longer available with the exception of a Sundays only Peakland Service.*

If the choice is otherwise, with a preference for continuing the walk down the dale, cross the bridge over the river and turn left downstream by the motor road for about ½ mile until coming to Milldale hamlet.

Here we recross the river again by means of a narrow twin-arched bridge — the Viator Bridge mentioned in *The Compleat Angler* — to resume our way by the riverside path again.

About ¾ mile downstream is the Dove Holes — two shallow caves — where we can, as an alternative, deviate from the dale by turning eastwards (left hand) for a stiff climb up to Hanson Grange by way of Nabs Dale and then continue to the New Inns Hotel at Alsop-en-le-Dale mentioned earlier.

Preferring to continue down the dale, however, we are soon in a tree-lined gorge.

About 300 yards downstream from the Dove Holes it is possible to recross the river again by a narrow tree-trunk bridge at the foot of Ilam Rock in order to explore Hall Dale on the Staffordshire side.

Retracing our steps and again continuing downstream, we pass innumerable rock formations of fantastic shapes on each side of the gorge—notably Lion's Head Rock, Reynard's Cave, Tissington Spires and the Twelve Apostles—before emerging at the Stepping Stones at the foot of Thorpe Cloud.

We can either cross by the Stepping Stones for a stroll as far as the Ilam-Thorpe road, or turn left uphill away from the river through Lin Dale, at the eastern end of Thorpe Cloud, to bring us out in Thorpe Village. At Thorpe there is an infrequent (dependent on the time of day) bus service into Ashbourne.

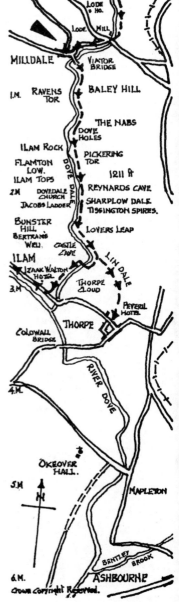

Milford, Chevin, Duffield

A SHORT and interesting walk, suitable for a pleasant summer evening, is over the Chevin, for there are some distant views of Belper and the Derwent Valley beyond worth absorbing when the air is still and the factories below are at rest.

Starting from the Strutt Arms at Milford, cross over the main Derby-Belper road and turn up Sunny Bank opposite.

Within a matter of some 50 yards from our starting point we are confronted with the choice of proceeding along Chevinside (on the right), or turning left for the stiff climb up Sunny Bank and on to the top of the Chevin. It is the latter route we are following.

The square-built tower near the top—as distinct from the smoke ventilator shafts—was built for surveying the route when the Chevin railway tunnel and Derwent Valley route were contructed during the last century.

With the golf course on either side of the track we are steadily climbing upwards until the route levels out shortly before we reach the high stone wall safety curtain of a disused firing range.

After proceeding along a level stretch for another ½ mile or so we double back on our route by way of a track which comes into our original path on the left hand.

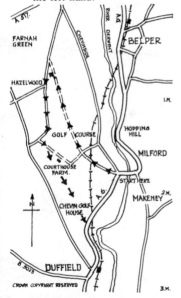

A short, steady climb brings us out at the rear of a covered service reservoir. There is a sunken, and somewhat rough, lane to the south of the reservoir which takes us down to the Hazelwood-Farnah Green road. Turn to the left and ignore the T-junction to Hazelwood on the right.

Carry on southwards down the road and where it dips steeply and bends to the right there is an opening on the left near the bottom of the hill. Turn in here and pass the farm buildings on the right and follow the path round the rear of some buildings about 100 yards in front.

Continuing forward along the hillside track for ½ mile, turn through the stile in the right hand boundary wall, about 100 yards short of Courthouse Farm. Proceed diagonally downfield to the left and join up with the boundary fence to the golf links.

This way eventually brings us into a lane running past the golf house, which we continue to follow to the main Duffield-Belper road.

Derby, Barrow-on-Trent, Swarkeston, Shelton Lock

A PLEASANT walk over Sinfin Moor from the Derby suburbs can be made into the Trent Valley and the villages of Barrow-on-Trent and Swarkeston, but this route is not recommended in wet weather.

Alight from the Shelton Lock bus at Boulton Lane and cross the road to Sinfin Lane (signposted 'Sinfin') and go down past the Church and take the first turn right past Morningside Close and continue to a farm, and turn left along a path to cross the railway in a few hundred yards. Follow the green path under the power lines to Red Wood, seen ahead. Cross the brook and follow the woodside and hedge to another brook, over which we follow the hedge and path, twisting through a small spinney. Continue down the same hedgeside to turn right along a cart track near the end of the second field. In 100 yards this turns left through a gateway to become a green lane.

Over the hill the lane becomes a good road as it drops into the Trent Valley. Crossing the canal, railway and new by-pass road, we enter Barrow-on-Trent and continue forward to the church. Leave the churchyard by the opposite gate and follow the lane to the river and a delightful group of cottages.

Here a signpost points to Swarkeston, across the fields and the last stile is found beside a farm. In the lane we turn right to the river bridge. Our way goes straight over the main road to a rough road on the river bank, but we should climb the bridge to see the 13th-century causeway, twisting and undulating across the valley.

Continuing along the river bank, we turn left to the church, where there are fine monuments to the Harpurs who lived close by. Across the field, behind the church, can be seen a recently renovated grandstand in the Balcony Field.

The lane crosses the main road again to Swarkeston Bubble, where the now derelict Derby Canal joined the Trent and Mersey Canal, used extensively by pleasure craft.

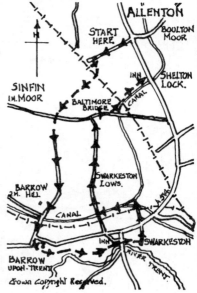

We follow the towpath left past the lock house to the next bridge, where we turn right up a lane. The farm of Swarkeston Lows takes its name from the burial mounds seen in the fields opposite. The result of excavations at the site by students and members of Derbyshire Archaeological Society may be seen at Derby Borough Museum.

Our road becomes a track, and through a gateway follows a hedge left to a green road, where we turn right to another canal bridge. Left along the derelict canal towpath brings us to Shelton Lock.

Repton, Bretby, Newton Solney

THE CHARM of historic Repton, with nearby valleys and low-rounded hills round Bretby, woods with hazel nuts, conkers and sweet chest-nuts—if you are lucky!—all combine to make this a delightful and easy walk in South Derbyshire.

The shaft of an ancient cross on circular steps, the Parish Church and renowned public school are within sight as we alight from the bus in the main street of Repton.

A fine arched gateway and the Guest House seen through it are almost all that is left of a Norman priory built on the site of a Saxon monastery, and now part of Repton School. Enter the church and see the wonderful Saxon crypt, all that is left of the monastery, where kings and princes were buried when Repton was the capital of Mercia. The modern gateway across the street leads to new school buildings.

We retrace our steps past the cross and continue through the village until, just past the Shakespeare Inn, we find a signpost marked Public Footpath beside the last new house on the left. Follow the path, which

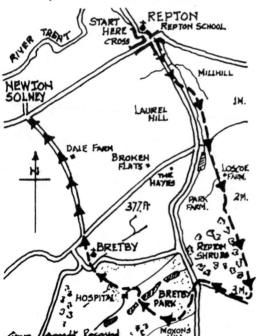

crosses a stream and ends in an open area of grass. Here stood an old mill and cottage mentioned in a previous edition of this booklet.

A stile is found to the right of the hedge seen ahead, and once over it the path follows further stiles up the valley in line with the hedge on the right. Two new stiles of concrete—one on each side of the stream and private— mark the route of the pipeline from the River Dove to Calke reservoir, near Melbourne. Our last stile leads into a road which falls steeply from the left to a tree-shaded bridge, a popular picnic spot with summer motorists.

But we soon leave them, for straight ahead we enter the

lane designated No Through Road for Motor Vehicles, which soon climbs between rocky banks. A backward glance shows the slender spire of Repton Church. At the first farm — Loscoe Farm — on the hilltop, the road makes a right turn to Park Farm, but we ignore this and continue forward down a pebbly cart track, which enters an open field and follows the hedge along the shallow valley bottom.

On the right the hillside is covered by Repton Shrubs, owned by the Forestry Commission and now reset with conifers. Ignoring the gate into the wood, we continue with the wood on our right to climb a hill straight ahead. Here one may pause and look back down one of those little known and secluded valleys in this part of Derbyshire, yet only a few miles from the mining district of Swadlincote, just over the hill southwards.

On the hilltop we join a narrow road and continue beside the wood to turn right at a junction about ½ mile on. Passing Greysich Farm there is another delightful view ahead as the lane drops steeply to the main road, where we turn right to cross a small bridge about 100 yards away.

Immediately over the bridge a signpost to Midway points up a steep lane to the left. At a new bungalow on the right a narrow path goes straight ahead with a wood on the right and glimpses across the valley to Greysich Farm, high on the hillside on the left. Down on the left the tree-lined stream has kept us company and the road undulates along the opposite hillside before disappearing over the shoulder of the hill towards Hartshorne.

We pass through a farm gate ahead and the path goes round the field and enters a wood on a well defined path which descends to a lane where we immediately turn right, re-entering the wood. The path can be followed if we note that it keeps parallel with the fence seen about 20 yards on the left, and when it turns deeper into the wood it is unmistakeable. A steep climb through the trees, then through a small gate and we are in the open — to follow a green path straight across a ploughed field to the crest of the hill, about 200 yards ahead.

This is Bretby Park, with open parkland dipping into the valley spread out before us. The path continues straight down the hillside towards the right of a deep plantation of firs to round the last shoulder of the hill, when the impressive pile of Bretby Hall suddenly looms into view across the lake.

Rebuilt in 1813, Bretby Hall replaced an earlier structure by Inigo Jones — a wonderful building set in a magnificent park. Once the home of the Earls of Chesterfield, it was fortified and plundered in the Civil War, and the "new" building, often visited by Disraeli, is now doing fine work as a hospital. The original hall is said to have been built from Bretby Castle, the site of which is indicated by a hummocky corner in the village.

Crossing the dam which forms part of a string of small lakes, we follow the track straight uphill to a plantation, which bears left round it to a gateway and the rear of the hall. Through the gateway we turn right down the drive, where in season there are usually conkers and sweet chestnuts.

A few hundred yards past the clock-towered building seen on the right a stile is found with a footpath heading downfield towards the low spire of Bretby Church. Over another stile we cross the road to pass the triangular green with covered pump (war memorial) and on up to the church.

To the right of the churchyard gate a smaller one leads into a field, where, keeping left beside the fence, we cross a stile. The path is undefined and we make a straight line up the open field towards the right side of a clump of trees on the hilltop, where a stile is seen on the right.

Crossing over, we aim downhill towards the centre of the bottom hedge, where a stile gives access to a road. A signpost here indicates three miles to Repton and 1½ miles to Newton Solney, where we may catch a bus home.

Markeaton Stones, Vicarwood, Mackworth, Kedleston

A^N interesting field walk near Derby is accessible from Markeaton Lane, on the outskirts of the town.

Enter Markeaton Lane from the Kedleston Road and take the first turn on the right, just beyond the bridge over the brook. Proceed past the farm on the left hand and continue for a further ¼ mile into open fields. Cross two fields by veering to the right before coming up to a farm road climbing the hillside to Vicarwood on the left. Turn leftwards up the track, which eventually runs parallel with a covert of trees on the right. On the far side of the wood, nestling in the valley below, is Kedleston Hall, but ramblers should not risk trespassing by deviating from the route.

A branch cart-track on the left leading downfield to Lower Vicarwood Farm will take us across the fields to Mackworth village, where we turn left down the road as far as Mackworth Vicarage. Here, we take to the fields again for a return to Markeaton Lane by way of Mackworth Church.

If we prefer to avoid the route down past Lower Vicarwood, continue forward for about a ¼ mile to Upper Vicarwood Farm and proceed through a gate on the left of the farm buildings. This route is very muddy in wet weather.

Continuing forward, however, we keep the woods to the right and proceed between the fence and the headland of plough until we join up with the Kirk Langley-Kedleston lane opposite Priestwood Farm. A left turn takes one to Kirk Langley, the right-hand direction fetching us up in the village of Kedleston.

While in Kedleston ramblers are conveniently situated for a visit to Kedleston Hall, the 18th-century residence of Viscount and Viscountess Scarsdale. The Hall is open to the public on Sundays during the spring and summer months.

A noble example of the work of Robert Adam, though not all the credit for the design can be ascribed to him, Kedleston Hall is a magnificent house with the Marble Hall the most outstanding of its many fine State apartments.

Melbourne, Staunton Harold Hall, Ticknall

IN the area south of Melbourne lies Staunton Harold Hall, now a
Cheshire Foundation Home for the Sick, and to the west is Ticknall and
the woods around Seven Spouts Hill — all linked with footpaths which
deserve to be more widely known.

Alighting from the bus in Melbourne at Potter Street, continue down
Church Street to the fine Norman church, noting the old tithe barn at the
west end and Melbourne Hall at the east.

Pass through the gate to Melbourne Pool, from which it is claimed the
stone from the long vanished castle was quarried, and on the left we see an
old mill, the hall and a yew tunnel.

Continue beside the lake and where the lane turns left a kissing gate is
found about 40 yards on the right. Go through the gate and head for the
top of the garden seen on our left, when a stile is seen straight ahead.
Cross over and follow the left edge of the field, beside a brook and then a

wood, and where the
wood ends follow the
hedge to its lowest
point. Cross a stile
here and head straight
up the hillside to a
gate seen on the top,
through which we
continue to a concrete
stile.

Follow the hedge
downhill and along-
side a wood to its
corner and cross to
trees in the valley
bottom ahead. Over
the brook, cross im-
mediately over the
fence on the right and
follow the right hedge
uphill to a lane. Turn
right and then left at
the main road to the
entrance to Staunton
Harold, about ½ mile
on the right.

Through the lodge
gates the drive soon
reveals a lovely pic-
ture of a hall, private
chapel and lake.
Through the orna-
mental gateway turn
left to the chapel,

63

noting wording around the parapet and a tablet over the west door. Regain the drive and follow the rough road left to pass behind the Hall past the stables and on down the long drive to the road at Heath End.

Turn left and then right at the next road junction, and after rounding an "S" bend a farm is seen on the right. About 100 yards on the same side pass through a small gate to cross two narrow fields, diagonally left, to a gateway seen on the corner of a wood. Continue alongside the wood, pass through two fields to cross a stream.

Proceed over a stile and cross an open field along a mound which curves left to meet a hedge. Three stiles lead into the valley bottom, where we cross a raised green track — a disused tramway which carried bricks and pottery from the industry which once flourished at Ticknall.

Straight ahead (uphill) another stile is seen and over it we make for the brick wall and follow it to the main road, turning right and right again at the Give Way sign. Ticknall Church lies up the lane on the left. Leave the churchyard by the other gate, cross the schoolyard, pass through a kissing gate and cross a small field. Chapel Street is seen across the road and we continue down this to a gate barring the road.

The well-known horseshoe bridge, which carried the old tramway mentioned previously, is seen spanning the main road in front. Enter the field on the left through a gate, and go straight up towards the second electricity pole to a small gate. The path runs along a hedgeside in line with the poles. Where the poles fork, follow the left row across the field to a gate in a wood.

Passing through the wood, our way goes down the open valley to follow the left boundary of a narrow wood, and, just past a cottage is a gate through which we pass.

The path drops steeply through a wood and over another stile makes a T junction with a green track. We turn right and once through the second gate we join a good road to turn right to the entrance to Ingleby Toft, about 200 yards ahead on the left.

Opposite, a Public Bridleway sign points down to a brook to continue uphill beside the boundary of denuded Robin Wood, passing through several fields to the Stanton-by-Bridge/Ticknall road. Crossing the road, we proceed to the main Derby/Melbourne road, where a bus stop will be found near the Francis Burdett Inn.

● The route maps, based upon the Ordnance Survey map with the sanction of the Controller of H.M. Stationery Office, have been drawn by Mr. C.H. Brown.

● Published by Derbyshire Countryside Ltd., Lodge Lane, Derby, and printed by Taylor Bloxham Ltd, Leicester.